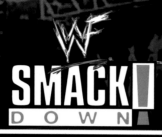

Welcome to WWF *SmackDown!™: Prima's Official Strategy Guide*. The Superstars of the World Wrestling Federation are all here. Stone Cold Steve Austin, Big Boss Man, Debra, Buh-Buh Ray, Chyna, Godfather, and a host of others. Thirty-six Superstars are packed into this awesome PlayStation game, and they're waiting for you. And there are tons of options. In Exhibition Mode, you can select from 12 different kinds of matches such as Hardcore and King of the Ring. In Season Mode you can ride your Superstar from the pre-season all the way to WrestleMania®. Plus you get Pay-Per-View (PPV) Mode to create your own special WWF event. WWF *SmackDown!™* has it all, and this guide gives you all of the strategies. You get complete move lists for each of the 36 Superstars of the WWF, plus tips on Exhibition, Season, Pay-Per-View, and Create-a-Superstar modes. It's all here. So are you ready to enter the squared circle? Can I get a Hell Yeah?

WWF *SmackDown!™* has it all. Are you ready for the start of a new season?

There are 12 different kinds of matches in WWF *SmackDown!™* Here Steve Blackman wins a Cage Match.

The lovely ladies of the WWF are in the game too. Here Debra has Tori against the turnbuckle in a Choke Hold.

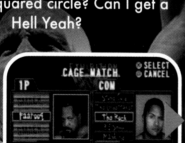

Pick any combination you want. WWF *SmackDown!™* has 36 Superstars to choose from.

D'Von Dudley gets Paul Bearer up into the air with a Suplex. All of the moves are here in WWF *SmackDown! ™* too.

You'll find weapons outside the ring. Use them to your advantage.

The Undertaker puts Stone Cold Steve Austin into a Darkness Pin.

Introduction

Before you step into the ring, you'll need to know a few things about the game. After all, you want to be the best when you take on your friends. Check out this section for a rundown of all the information you need to know to become the next rising star in the World Wrestling Federation.

Basic Controls

Action	Control
Pause Game	START
Move Superstar	D-Pad
Striking Attacks	×
Irish Whip to Ropes	●
Grapple Attacks	D-Pad + ●
Reverse/Counter	■
Run	▲
Climb Turnbuckle	D-Pad + ▲
Climb out of Ring	D-Pad + R1
Slide into Ring	▲
Tag Partner	R1
Pin Opponent	↓ + ●
Pick Up Weapon	R1
Attack with Weapon	×

Here you are on your way into the ring of the WWF. Do your home-work with this guide to find out all of the moves and how to win.

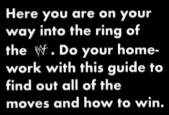

The first rule of thumb is to wear down your opponent's defenses. Striking Attacks (×) can do that.

When your opponent is on the ground, take advantage of it.

You'll need to get to a pin count of three to win the match by fall. You can also get counted out of the ring or get knocked out.

Weapons

What would WWF SmackDown!™ be without some weapons? Pick one up by pressing R1, then press × to use your newly acquired tool. You can do lots of damage to your opponent with weapons.

Press R1 to pick up a weapon.

Press × to strike your opponent with the weapon.

Picking Your Superstar

First pick out your Superstar. You also can decide how much energy your character has at the start of the match and how high his or her energy can get during a challenge.

By changing the minimum and max-imum energy but-tons, you then figure out if you need to handicap the match.

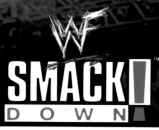

Third Man In

Be careful! Sometimes an outsider will come down the ramp and join the meleé for one side or the other.

Finishing Moves

Watch the upper left corner of the screen. When you see the word *SMACK!*, your Superstar is ready for a finishing move.

Climb the Turnbuckle

When your opponent is stunned, climb the turnbuckle using D-Pad + ▲.

Press L1 to start the finishing move. You'll see the word *SMACK!* flash across the screen in large letters as the move begins.

Press ✗ to attack your opponent. Maybe with a ...

Here the Big Boss Man is about to finish off X-Pac.

... Flying Elbow.

Finishing moves are a great way to put away your opponent.

Ready for a single match? Well, WWF *SmackDown!*™ has enough choices to keep you occupied. There are 12 different kinds of exhibition matches: Single Match, Tag Match, Handicap, Battle Royal, Royal Rumble®, King of the Ring®, Hardcore, Anywhere Fall, Cage Match, Survival Match, Special Referee, and I Quit. Each of those matches has a different way to win. Check out this section for a quick breakdown.

Single Match

The Single Match is your chance to battle the computer or a friend in a basic match. You have the choice of playing with or without the aid of a manager.

Work over your opponent until you can get that pin! With moves such as Piledrivers and the Mounted Punch, you'll be all set to deliver the Undertaker's Darkness Pin here.

Tag Match

Pit four opponents against each other in the squared circle. You can play by yourself or with up to three friends (if you have a multi-tap that is). When you get to the corner, press R1 to tag off to your teammate.

In a tag match, it's two-on-two action. It starts out fair, but after tagging out R1, you can have two-on-one in the ring.

Handicap

What? One-on-one isn't enough of a challenge for you? Then head on over to a Handicap Match and play either one-on-two or one-on-three.

Two-on-one isn't exactly fair. Try to work over one wrestler at a time, but don't ignore the other one—you'll get creamed that way! Grapple with one while you take time out to keep the second or third opponent at a distance. You may lose your first couple of Handicap Matches before you find the balance.

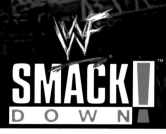

Battle Royal

The Battle Royal is a crowd of activity. Four Superstars enter the ring and only one emerges victorious. To come out on top, concentrate on one opponent. Work him over and then go for the pin. The other way to win is by knocking out all three opponents. You want to be the last man standing in this bout.

Four Superstars enter the squared circle for a massive fight.

Concentrate on one opponent. After pinning one opponent, you can move to the next one.

Royal Rumble®

In the Royal Rumble, you start with four people in the ring, but more enter as people are thrown out of the ring. Pace yourself and you should do fine in this super match.

The Royal Rumble starts out like a Battle Royal...

...but after someone is thrown out, a fresh Superstar takes his or her place until you are the last one standing.

King of the Ring®

To be the King of the Ring, you need to survive three matches. Fight it like a normal bout and you will do fine.

You have to work your way through this mini-tournament bracket to be crowned King of the Ring.

Here The Undertaker gets Hardcore Holly in a Choke Hold to win the match.

Hardcore

In a Hardcore Match, you start out with a weapon in hand. Press R1 to pick up the weapon (if you drop it), X to attack with it, and R1 to throw it at your opponent. Head outside the ring without fear of a count out.

You start out with a weapon in a Hardcore Match, but there are more outside the ring. You can even grab the steps to smash your opponent.

Anywhere Fall

In an Anywhere Fall competition, the Superstars can wander about the W SmackDown!™ venue for the fight. Go up the ramp or even backstage. Have fun grappling outside of the squared circle for a change. There are tons of fun weapons out there, so go get them and then get the pin for the victory. Also, new weapons will become available to you as you smash your opponent into different objects.

To get backstage, you need to get your opponent up the ramp. Execute an Irish Whip ● from this spot to move ...

...to the entry-way!

Execute an Irish Whip ● here and you'll go further behind the scenes of W SmackDown!™

This is the next area you enter. There are lots of weapons to do battle with backstage.

Another Irish Whip ● from here and you are near the ambulance and the parking garage.

Look, more weapons!

And finally a pin.

Cage Match

You'll have to climb your way out of the ring to win a Cage Match. Press any direction plus R1 to climb up the cage. Make sure your opponent is down and out before making your attempt though, or your opponent can knock you off the cage. If your enemy is climbing out, run over to that section of the cage and press X or ● to shake him or her down. Once on the cage, you need to press ↑ to climb farther, or press R1 to climb back down.

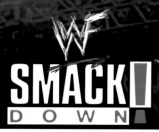

Rough your opponent up, then head up the cage. You've got to be the first to get over the top to win one of these bouts.

Survival Match

In a Survival Match, you are given the choice of a 3-Way or 4-Way Dance. Anything goes in this combination of the Handicap and Hardcore matches. Be the first person to pin or K.O. an opponent to win.

It's every man for himself in a Survival Match.

Attack one opponent until you get a K.O. or a pin.

Special Referee

Special Referee allows you to assign a Superstar as a referee for your match. The referee can be computer controlled or human controlled. The referee will count slowly or quickly, depending on who he likes or dislikes in the match. If a human player is controlling the referee, tap L2 for each count. If the referee isn't counting fast enough for you, take it out on him with a Body Slam or a Suplex!

This is just like any other match, except the referee is a Superstar of the World Wrestling Federation.

He can count faster or slower depending on whether he likes the person getting pinned. Be careful, you can be had by a quick three count in a match like this.

I Quit

The only way to win this match is by submission. You'll have to work your opponent all over the arena. Get your opponent out of the ring and up the ramp if you want to go backstage. This will be a long, drawn-out match. The only way to win is if your opponent admits defeat in the microphone.

When your opponent is on the mat and ready to submit, grab the microphone and press ↓+●.

The Matches

Create a PPV gives you the chance to create your own Pay-Per-View Event. Head to the menu and select up to six matches. Choose any combination of the following for your special event:

You can create 6 different matches.

- *Single Match*
- *Single Match with Manager*
- *Tag Match*
- *One-on-Two*
- *One-on-Three*
- *Battle Royal*
- *Hardcore Match*
- *Anywhere Match*
- *Cage Match*
- *3-Way Dance*
- *4-Way Dance*
- *Special Referee*
- *I Quit Match*

Once you have picked the kind of match, select the Superstars, whether there's a title on the line, and whether you or the computer will control the opponents.

Ratings

Pay-Per-View Events are all about the ratings. Head on over to the Audience Ranking number to find out how your event did. So how do you get a high ranking number? Give the fans what they want, such as Title Matches and lots of action in the ring. Counters, reversals, and big finishing moves will keep the fans riveted to the TV. Get four or more people into the ring (Tag Matches, 4-Way Dances, and Battle Royals) to get the fans to tune in.

You can see the audience ranking.

After the match, you see the Audience Ranking number. Pay-Per-View Events need strong ratings.

When all six matches are finished, you can check out how your event ranked compared to other Pay-Per-View Events

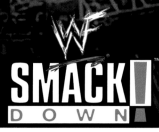
You can also check out how individual parts of your match ranked in terms of the Audience Ratings.

3-Way Dances are a good way to get people to tune in. The more people in the ring, the better.

Fans love Title Matches too. Keep an eye out for interference though.

Behind the scenes action is another draw. Put an Anywhere Fall Match in there and head out of the ring.

Tori sets up for a SmackDown!™ move, a Tori Suplex. Fans like big finishing moves, so give them the action they want.

WWF *SmackDown!™* gives you the ultimate test as the newest Talent in the ring. Create your Superstar, enter the pre-season, then take on the WWF in full-season competition. Can you rise all the way from last-ranked up to the World Wrestling Federation Champion? Now you can find out.

The Pre-Season

Check out the next section for a description of how to create your Superstar.

Set up all the character's attributes before heading into the pre-season.

Once you have created a Superstar, you need to start out in the pre-season. Pre-season starts just after *WrestleMania®* and runs through the next *WrestleMania®* (one year later). Your Jobber can go through the pre-season once, while you can play multiple seasons with the Superstar.

When you win a match in the pre-season, you gain points to contribute to your Talent's abilities. Different matches are worth more points to your Superstar. Winning a single match is worth a small number of points, but winning a Battle Royal is worth nearly double. The matches and your opponents are picked at random. As you increase your ability points, more moves will become available to assign to your Jobber.

The pre-season gives you a chance to practice all of your moves, such as this Suplex. Once you complete a pre-season, your Jobber is ready for the real thing.

After you win a match, you are given...

...more points to increase your Superstar's attributes.

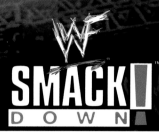

Pre-season and season events include the WWF *SummerSlam™* Pay-Per-View.

The matches are picked random[ly] Unless you're really on your ga[me] this one's not fair! It's only the p[re-]season for your Jobber and you have to square off against WWF Champion Big Show.

Alliances

After some matches, you see a cut scene where one of the WWF Superstars speaks to your newly created Jobber. In the first conversation, the Superstar gives you advice or congratulates you after a big win. After the Superstar is finished speaking, you are given the choice to respond. You can either thank the Superstar, or tell him to shut up.

How you answer the question will determine the allegiances and rivalries your Superstar will have in his career. Say "thank you," and perhaps that Superstar will help you out in a match. In later conversations the Superstar will solicit your help to ambush someone backstage. If you tell the Superstar to shut up, you've made an enemy for your entire Superstar career.

Thanks,
Shut up!

After a match, Superstars approach your newly created character. After receiving some advice, you may have the option to respond. Say thanks, or tell them to shut up.

Big Show seems really happy with Shaft now.

If you say 'thank you', you'll have a potential ally.

Along the way you are bound to lose a match or two.

So what were the Hardyz thinking? That you'd be polite if you just lost? So tell them so!

Thanks,
Shut up!

Jeff Hardy is really pissed off.

OK, they're mad at you, but you were mad at them. Now you're even.

PRE-SEASON MODE
CHARACTER.   SELECT / CANCEL
Power Attack
Jeff Hardy +
Hardy Boyz +

This superstar is good with powerful attacks.

At some point during the pre-season, you will be presented with a screen such as this, where you can view the character elements your Superstar has been able to attain.

Season

Once you've gotten through the pre-season, it's time to move to the regular season. Each month WF SmackDown!™ randomly picks the matches. Win the match and you earn ranking points for your Jobber. Lose the match and you lose ranking points. At the end of the month, you can check the rankings to find out which championship belts you are eligible for. The season ends at the end of WrestleMania®. Once the season is over, you can continue with your Superstar in a new season.

During the season you'll face all kinds of matches, such as Hardcore...

...Tag Team matches...

...and matches at events such as Raw is War®, Royal Rumble®, and WrestleMania®.

Championship Belts

Belt	Ranking Needed	Gender
World Wrestling Federation Champion	1–5	Male
Intercontinental Champion	1–10	Both
Tag Team Champion	All are eligible	Both
European Champion	1–20	Both
Hardcore Champion	1–20	Both
Federation Women's Champion	All are eligible	Female

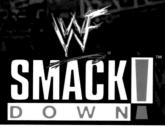

Prima's Official Strategy Guide

TITLE HOLDER LIST
⊘ SELECT
⊘ CANCEL

World Wrestling
Federation : Big Show
Intercontinental : Chris Jericho
Tag Team : The Rock
: Mankind
European : Val Venis
Hardcore : Big Boss Man
Woman's : Tori

To see who holds each belt in the WF, check out the Title Holder List.

RANKING
⊘ SELECT
⊘ CANCEL

RANK	NAME	POINTS
9TH	Triple H	43
10TH	Road Dogg	42
11TH	Mr. Ass	40
12TH	Edge	40
13TH	Val Venis	38
14TH	The Undertaker	37
15TH	Ken Shamrock	37
16TH	Gangrel	31

Want to compete for one of those belts? Then check out the current point rankings and compare your ranking to the table above.

If you select a Superstar from the ranking menu, you can see stats on all of the Talent.

RANKING
⊘ SELECT
⊘ CANCEL

RANK	NAME	POINTS
1ST	Stone Cold	77

THE TOTAL NUMBER OF MATCHES
PARTICIPATION (%)   35.8%
VICTORIES (%)   20.6%
A NUMBER OF MATCHES   58
WIN   12
LOST   4
EVEN   0

The alliances you make in the pre-season carry over into the regular season. Your friends come to your aid when you need it.

W *SmackDown!*™ comes with 36 Superstars ready for action. But what if 36 isn't enough for you? Create your version of talent to capture all of the titles in the World Wrestling Federation! You've got a lot of room to experiment with your newly created Superstar: you can adjust the profile, personality, and appearance. But you don't have to go through all of the steps at once. Save your work and come back to it at a later date.

Create-a-Superstar allows you to make your own Superstar.

Give the Talent a name and fill out his or her profile first...

...then work on appearance...

...and then on his or her personality.

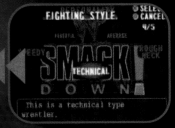

When you're done, you can head to the ring to challenge the best the W has to offer.

Profile and Appearance

The Profile section is pretty straightforward. You have to give your newly created character the basics. Name, nickname, age, sex, and native place tell the W fans about the character. Favorite Star lets you pick whom your athlete will align with, and the Entrance Movie lets you select a video for your ring entrance. Complete the Profile section by selecting Completion, then head over to Appearance. Now that we know who your up-and-coming Superstar is, we need to know what he or she looks like.

W *SmackDown!*™ gives you a ton of options when it comes to selecting your Jobber's look. You will have the following to choose from after unlocking the hidden Superstar appearances:

- More than 70 head styles
- More than 70 upper body styles
- More than 90 lower body styles
- Sliders for height and weight
- Four different skin tones
- 20 different weapons

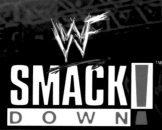

Personality

The Personality menu has five different areas you must fill out to make your entry into the WWF complete: Fighting Style, Ability, Character, Logic, and Moves.

Fighting Style

Choose from five different Fighting Styles:

- *Average*
- *Powerful*
- *Speedy*
- *Technical*
- *Rough Neck*

Ability

Your new Superstar has 12 different attributes that define his or her ability. You can select the amount of damage your character can do and determine the kinds of available moves. You've got 70 points to divvy up among the categories. Tweak them until you get the right mix for the moves you want to accomplish. After increasing your ability points, more moves will be available to give to your Jobber.

Here is the menu for the Ability section of Create-a-Superstar. The little graph on the left tells you how strong your character is in the four categories.

Character

The Character menu allows you to pick another level of specialization for your new Superstar. Pick only one of the skills from the list and your player will have a small advantage in the category you pick. Do you want a little bit more powerful attack? Want an edge in Hardcore Matches? You've got a pretty long list to pick from.

Logic

On the Logic submenu, you get the opportunity to pick two different specializations for your character. Will your character be good at Punching and Kicking, Grappling, Aerial Moves, Ground Moves, Using Weapons, or have an average balance? You make all the decisions here.

This is the Logic menu. You get to pick two different specializations for your character.

To complete your character's moves, fill out this chart. Fill in the blanks, then use these pages as a "cheat sheet" for your Superstar.

Moves

Action	Control
Facing the Opponent	
Irish Whip to Ropes	●
_____	↑+●
_____	→+●
_____	↓+●
_____	←+●
_____	✕
_____	↑+✕
_____	→+✕
_____	↓+✕
_____	←+✕
Facing a Groggy Opponent	
_____	↑+●
_____	→+●
_____	↓+●
_____	←+●
Behind a Groggy Opponent	
Irish Whip to Ropes	●
_____	↑+●
_____	→+●
_____	↓+●
_____	←+●
Opponent on Mat	
Upper Body	
Raise Opponent (front)	●
Raise Opponent (behind)	●,●
Pin Opponent	↓+●
_____	↑+●
_____	←+●
_____	→+●
_____	✕
_____	↑+✕
_____	→+✕
_____	↓+✕
_____	←+✕

Action	Control
Lower Body	
Raise Opponent From Mat	●
Pin Opponent	↓+●
_____	↑+●
_____	→+●
_____	←+●
Turnbuckle Moves	
Facing Opponent	
Irish Whip to Ropes	●
_____	←+●/→+●
_____	↓+●/↑+●
Behind Opponent	
Irish Whip to Ropes	●
_____	←+●/→+●
_____	↓+●/↑+●
Opponent Sitting in Lower Turnbuckle	
_____	●
_____	←+●/→+●
_____	↓+●/↑+●
_____	▲+✕
Rope Attacks	
Knock Over/Through Rope	✕
Dive Through Ropes	▲+■+✕
Jump Over Ropes	D-Pad +▲+✕
Turnbuckle Attacks	
Opponent Standing	
_____	✕
_____	←+✕/→+✕
_____	↓+✕/↑+✕
Opponent on Mat	
_____	✕
_____	←+✕/→+✕
_____	↓+✕/↑+✕

Running Attacks

Facing Opponent

_____ ●

_____ ←+● / →+●

_____ ↓+● / ↑+●

_____ ✕

_____ ←+✕ / →+✕

_____ ↓+✕ / ↑+✕

Behind Opponent

_____ ●

_____ ←+● / →+●

_____ ↓+● / ↑+●

Running Counterattacks

Opponent Running

_____ ●

_____ ←+● / →+●

_____ ↓+● / ↑+●

Finishing Moves

Full SmackDown!™ Meter

On Top Rope   [L1]

Facing Groggy Opponent   [L1]

Behind Groggy Opponent   [L1]

Opponent in Turnbuckle   [L1]

Opponent on Mat   [L1]

Based on the abilities you picked, your new character will have certain moves to choose from.

Does your new character have what it takes to become one of the Superstars of the WWF? Step into the squared circle and give it a go.

But be careful, Stone Cold Steve Austin and the others are a tough bunch.

Keep at it. This Suplex is the beginning of the end of this match.

This Scoop Slam puts the icing on the cake.

And you're the winner.

WF *SmackDown!*™ gives you 36 Superstars to choose from. If that's not enough, you've got Create-a-Superstar with tons of different body parts to make your own. Still not enough? Well, then there are the Hidden Superstars. As you move through Season Mode in WF *SmackDown!*™ you can unlock these Hidden Superstars. Once you've completed the necessary task, go back to Create-a-Superstar and that person's body parts are available. You'll have to enter all of the other data (name, moves, abilities) on your own.

The Hidden Superstars/Extra Ability Points

Superstar	Unlocked by
Pre-Season Mode	
Wealth	Complete 1 pre-season
European Title+ ability	Complete 2 pre-seasons
Women's Title+ ability	Complete 3 pre-seasons
Tournament+ ability	Complete 4 pre-seasons
Hardcore Title+ ability	Complete 5 pre-seasons
IC Title+ ability	Complete 6 pre-seasons
Tag Title+ ability	Complete 7 pre-seasons
Title Match+ ability	Complete 8 pre-seasons
Pre-Season Skip	Complete 10 pre-seasons
Blue Meanie	Stage 6/House Show 3B
Stevie Richards	Stage 5/House Show 3A
Stone Cold Steve Austin (alternate outfit)	Stage 58/House show ED1
The Rock (alternate outfit)	Stage 61/House show ED4
Stephanie McMahon	Stage 65/House show ED8
Season Mode	
Ivory	Complete 1 season
Prince Albert	Complete 2 seasons
Jacqueline	Complete 3 seasons
Viscera	Complete 4 seasons
80 ability points	Complete 5 seasons
Mideon	Complete 6 seasons
Gerald Brisco	Complete 7 seasons
Pat Patterson	Complete 8 seasons
90 ability points	Complete 10 seasons
100 ability points	Complete 20 seasons

Note: You can unlock more than one item at a time in the Pre-Season mode. You will usually receive Stevie Richards the first time through. If your Win/Loss ratio is superb, then you will receive Blue Meanie instead. Your created Superstar will perform better in match types with a "+" sign.

Pre-Season Mode allows you to unlock three Superstars and two alternate outfits.

Win the match in the fifth month (House Show)...

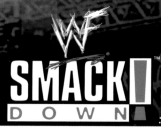

...and you'll be able to create a Superstar...

...that looks just like Blue Meanie! Lose the match and *SmackDown!™* unlocks Stevie Richards instead.

By doing Stage 58, House show ED1, you have access to Stone Cold Steve Austin in an alternate costume.

And by doing Stage 61, House show ED4, you get a more casual Rock in sunglasses and sweatpants.

Add Stephanie McMahon to the list of Superstars you can create by doing Stage 65, House show ED8.

Gain access to the lovely Jacqueline by completing 3 seasons.

And after 6 seasons, the body parts of Mideon the Seer are available in Create a Superstar.

Make your own version Viscera by completing 4 seasons.

Al Snow

Height: 6'0"
Weight: 234 lbs.
From: Lima, OH
Favorite Quote: "What does everybody want?"
Finishing Move: Snow Plow

BIOGRAPHY

Right after, "Do you smell what The Rock is cookin'?" the question WWF fans most like to hear has to be, "What does everybody want?" The answer is, of course, Al Snow's inanimate sidekick, HEAD.

There is no doubt that Al Snow and HEAD are a wildly entertaining duo, as many of their "conversations" have to be considered Federation classics, but the most disturbing thing about HEAD is that people focus on it so much that they take the person behind it for granted.

Lost in the shuffle of the euphoria that HEAD provides is the fact that Al Snow is one of the most talented Superstars on the roster. With Snow Plows, Hurracanranas off the barricade, and enough hardcore ability to fill a killer whale, Al Snow is an amazing athlete to watch.

And let's never forget that Al Snow is definitely not right in the, well, head (as if carrying around a mannequin doesn't already tell you this). He's got no problem fighting in a dress, beating himself over the noggin with a chair, or dragging his opponent outside to fight in a blizzard.

No matter what the conditions are—a Hardcore match, a comedy routine, or a spin on the psychologist's couch—Al Snow is definitely a good person to have on your side.

Moves

ACTION	CONTROL
Facing the Opponent	
Irish Whip to Ropes	●
Scissors Sweep	↓+●
Scoop Slam	←+●
Suplex	↑+●
Shoulder Breaker	→+●
Snap Jab	✕
Shuffle Side Kick	↓+✕
Toe Kick	←+✕
Boss Man Uppercut	↑+✕
Chop	→+✕
Facing the Groggy Opponent	
Jackknife Powerbomb	↓+●
DDT	←+●
Piledriver	↑+●
Hurracanrana	→+●
Behind the Opponent	
Irish Whip to Ropes	●
Diving Reverse DDT	↓+●
Back Drop	←+●
Reverse Brainbuster	↑+●
Bulldog	→+●
Opponent on Mat	
Upper Body	
Raise Opponent	●
Mahistorol Cradle	↑+●
Mounted Punch	→+●
Mounted Punch	←+●
Angry Stomp	✕
Elbow Drop	↓+✕
Angry Stomp	←+✕
Elbow Drop	↑+✕
Angry Stomp	→+✕
Lower Body	
Raise Opponent	●
Kick to Leg	↑+●
Knee Stomp	→+●
Texas Cloverleaf	←+●
Turnbuckle Moves	
Facing Opponent	
Irish Whip to Ropes	●
Choke	←+●/→+●
Frankensteiner	↓+●/↑+●
Behind Opponent	
Irish Whip to Ropes	●
Super Back Drop	←+●/→+●
Super Back Drop	↓+●/↑+●
Opponent Sitting in Lower Turnbuckle	
Raise Opponent	●
Choke	←+●/→+●
Choke	↓+●/↑+●
Clothesline	▲+✕
Turnbuckle Attacks	
Opponent Standing	
Double Axe Handle	✕
Double Axe Handle	←+✕/→+✕
Double Axe Handle	↓+✕/↑+✕
Opponent on Mat	
Elbow Drop	✕
Diving Moonsault	←+✕/→+✕
Diving Moonsault	↓+✕/↑+✕
Running Attacks	
Facing Opponent	
Neckbreaker	●
Spear	←+●/→+●
Spear	↓+●/↑+●
Clothesline	✕
Shoulder Block	←+✕/→+✕
Shoulder Block	↓+✕/↑+✕
Behind Opponent	
School Boy	●
School Boy	←+●/→+●
School Boy	↓+●/↑+●
Running Counterattacks—Opponent Running	

DID YOU KNOW?

Al Snow owns a gym in Ohio.

Shuffle Side Kick

↓ + ✕

in front of opponent

Monkey Toss

●

opponent running at you

Mahistorol Cradle

↑ + ●

opponent on mat

Snow Plow

L1

Al Snow & HEAD

HELP ME!!

Big Boss Man

Height: 6'6"
Weight: 355 lbs.
From: Cobb County, GA
Favorite Quote: "You're gonna serve hard time!"
Finishing Move: Boss Man Slam
Career Highlights: Tag Team Champion, Hardcore Champion

BIOGRAPHY

If you want to trace the evolution of the World Wrestling Federation over the past 15 years, there is perhaps no better subject to analyze than the Big Boss Man. During his first run with the WF, a much heftier Boss Man relied heavily on his gimmick (a "good" cop looking to put the "bad guys" away) to get over with the fans.

When he returned to the Federation, a physically fit Big Boss Man knew it was going to take more than a gimmick to make it this time around. Slimmed down, toned up, and much more agile, the Georgia native displayed aspects of his ability that no one had ever seen before. The most obvious of these were his "hardcore talents." While competing for, and eventually winning, the WF Hardcore Championship, the Big Boss Man took part in some of the most incredible matches the division had ever seen. With a number of healthy title reigns, the Boss Man became one of the most successful Hardcore Champions the WF has ever seen.

Outside of the ring, the Boss Man displayed many new abilities as well. Developing into the consummate entertainer, the Big Boss Man had you laughing out loud as he cooked Al Snow's dog, but had you seething with anger during his run as Mr. McMahon's "head of security."

We don't know about you, but we're looking to make quick friends with anyone who's well over 300 pounds, loves to get hardcore, and always carries around a nightstick.

Moves	
ACTION	**CONTROL**
Facing the Opponent	
Irish Whip to Ropes	●
Manhattan Drop	↓+●
Headlock and Punch	←+●
Eye Rake	↑+●
Side Buster	→+●
Toe Kick	✕
Boss Man Uppercut	↓+✕
Chop	←+✕
Double Axe Handle	↑+✕
Austin Punches	→+✕
Facing the Groggy Opponent	
Jackknife Powerbomb	↓+●
Rib Breaker	←+●
Stomach Crusher	↑+●
Pendulum Backbreaker	→+●
Behind the Opponent	
Irish Whip to Ropes	●
Atomic Drop	↓+●
Back Drop	←+●
Sleeper Hold	↑+●
Diving Reverse DDT	→+●
Opponent on Mat	
Upper Body	
Raise Opponent	●
Sleeper Hold	↑+●
Reverse Chin Lock	→+●
Camel Clutch	←+●
Angry Stomp	✕
Elbow Drop	↓+✕
Angry Stomp	←+✕
Elbow Drop	↑+✕
Angry Stomp	→+✕
Lower Body	
Raise Opponent	●
Kick to Leg	↑+●
Toss	→+●
Kick to Groin	←+●
Turnbuckle Moves	
Facing Opponent	
Irish Whip to Ropes	●
Mudhole Stomping	←+●/→+●
Foot Choke	↓+●/↑+●
Behind Opponent	
Irish Whip to Ropes	●
Super Back Drop	←+●/→+●
Super Back Drop	↓+●/↑+●
Opponent Sitting in Lower Turnbuckle	
Raise Opponent	●
Choke	←+●/→+●
Choke	↓+●/↑+●
Shoulder Block	▲+✕
Turnbuckle Attacks	
Opponent Standing	
Double Axe Handle	✕
Double Axe Handle	←+✕/→+✕
Double Axe Handle	↓+✕/↑+✕
Opponent on Mat	
Elbow Drop	✕
Elbow Drop	←+✕/→+✕
Elbow Drop	↓+✕/↑+✕
Running Attacks	
Facing Opponent	
Neckbreaker	●
Neckbreaker	←+●/→+●
Neckbreaker	↓+●/↑+●
Clothesline	✕
Back Elbow Attack	←+✕/→+✕
Back Elbow Attack	↓+✕/↑+✕
Behind Opponent	
Bulldog	●
Bulldog	←+●/→+●
Bulldog	↓+●/↑+●
Running Counterattacks—Opponent Running	
Monkey Toss	●
Boss Man Sidewalk Slam	←+●/→+●
Boss Man Sidewalk Slam	↓+●/↑+●

DID YOU KNOW?
An active community member, the Big Boss Man is always involved with a numbe
different charities at any given time.

Headlock an Punch

←+●

in front of opponent

Manhattan Drop

↓+●

in front of opponent

Boss Man Attack

←+●/→+●/↑+●/↓+

opponent on the rop

Boss Man Sidewalk Slam

L1

BIG BOSS MAN
Servin' Hard Time!

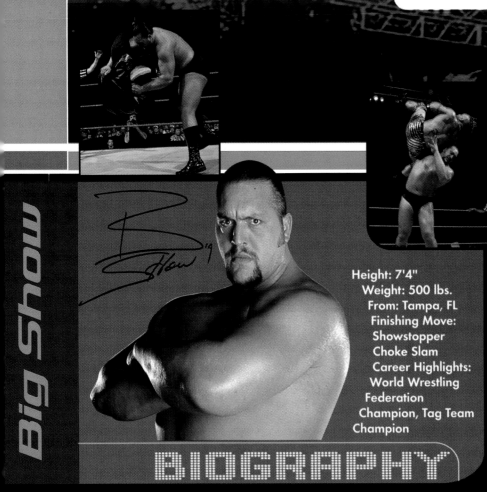

Big Show

Height: 7'4"
Weight: 500 lbs.
From: Tampa, FL
Finishing Move:
Showstopper
Choke Slam
Career Highlights:
World Wrestling Federation Champion, Tag Team Champion

BIOGRAPHY

Although being 7'4" and 500 pounds has many advantages (dunking a basketball without leaving the ground, never losing your lunch to the school bully), it also has a downside. Other than having a difficult time finding a loaner ball at the bowling alley, the problem with being so huge is that you have to figure out a way to make all of your appearances—especially your first one—as intimidating as your size.

Armed with the knowledge of how strong first impressions can be, WF officials and the Big Show must have spent many a night trying to figure out the best way to introduce him to the fans when he finally debuted in the Federation a little more than a year ago. And then *bang!* What better way to burst on the scene, than to burst on the scene?

So all the Big Show did on his first night was break through the canvas, pull himself up through the ring, and throw a Stone Cold Steve Austin fastball right through a steel cage. Big Show didn't stop there; in the coming months he lifted the entire ring because he was having one of those days, choke slammed The Undertaker straight to hell and flipped a car that nearly ended Hardcore Holly's days as a super heavyweight. And did we mention he won the W Tag Team Title and W Championship?

If the Big Show's first year as a World Wrestling Federation Superstar is any indication of how the rest of his career will go, it appears as if he is going to lift a lot of really heavy things...and win even more gold in the process!

Moves	
ACTION	**CONTROL**
Facing the Opponent	
Irish Whip to Ropes	●
Choke Toss	↓+●
Hard Scoop Slam	←+●
Pendulum Backbreaker	↑+●
Side Buster	→+●
Chop	×
Clothesline	↓+×
Big Boot	←+×
Double Axe Handle	↑+×
Body Punch	→+×
Facing the Groggy Opponent	
Jackknife Powerbomb	↓+●
Strong Head Butt	←+●
Body Press Drop	↑+●
Bearhug	→+●
Behind the Opponent	
Irish Whip to Ropes	●
Atomic Drop	↓+●
Full Nelson Slam	←+●
Sleeper Hold	↑+●
Turn Facing Front	→+●
Opponent on Mat	
Upper Body	
Raise Opponent	●
Camel Clutch	↑+●
Darkness Choke	→+●
Mounted Punch	←+●
Angry Stomp	×
Elbow Drop	↓+×
Angry Stomp	←+×
Elbow Drop	↑+×
Angry Stomp	→+×
Lower Body	
Raise Opponent	●
Boston Crab	↑+●
Kick to Leg	→+●
Knee Stomp	←+●
Turnbuckle Moves	
Facing Opponent	
Irish Whip to Ropes	●
Choke	←+●/→+●
Mudhole Stomping	↓+●/↑+●
Behind Opponent	
Irish Whip to Ropes	●
Super Back Drop	←+●/→+●
Super Back Drop	↓+●/↑+●
Opponent Sitting in Lower Turnbuckle	
Raise Opponent	●
Foot Choke	←+●/→+●
Foot Choke	↓+●/↑+●
Shoulder Block	▲+×
Turnbuckle Attacks	
Opponent Standing	
Double Axe Handle	×
Front Dropkick	←+×/→+×
Front Dropkick	↓+×/↑+×
Opponent on Mat	
Elbow Drop	×
Elbow Drop	←+×/→+×
Elbow Drop	↓+×/↑+×
Running Attacks	
Facing Opponent	
Neckbreaker	●
Neckbreaker	←+●/→+●
Neckbreaker	↓+●/↑+●
Shoulder Block	×
Dropkick	←+×/→+×
Dropkick	↓+×/↑+×
Behind Opponent	
School Boy	●
School Boy	←+●/→+●
School Boy	↓+●/↑+●
Running Counterattacks—Opponent Running	
Monkey Toss	●
Shoulder Back Toss	←+●/→+●
Shoulder Back Toss	↓+●/↑+●

Jackknife Powerbomb

↓ + ●

in front of groggy opponent

Neckbreaker

●

running to opponent, front

Dropkick

→ + ● / ← + ●

running at opponent

Showstopper

L1

Bradshaw

Bradshaw

Height: 6'6"
Weight: 290 lbs.
Finishing Move:
   Clothesline from Hell
Career Highlights:
   Tag Team
   Champion

BIOGRAPHY

It's no secret that throughout his illustrious World Wrestling Federation career, Bradshaw has worn many different hats. Although his physical appearance may have changed a bit over the past few years, the one thing that has remained constant is that he's a definitive "@#$-kicker."

Try and explain the concept of sports-entertainment to one of Bradshaw's opponents and he'll show a dozen bruises and lumps that prove a different theory. Never one to hide his love for getting physical, Bradshaw has made a career out of "looking for a fight."

There's no doubt that as long as he's been in the WF, Bradshaw has always threatened to rip your head off with each clothesline and tear a hole in your chest with each forearm, but it wasn't until he teamed up with Faarooq that fans started getting behind him.

And the reason for this is simple.

Alongside Faarooq, Bradshaw spent a lot of time hanging out at bars and picking fights with random strangers. He was finally given a forum where he could take advantage of his above-average ability to cut a promo. Put in a setting that was familiar to him (and one that always wins fan support)—the bar—Bradshaw only had to be himself. Given that opportunity, there was no doubt the fans would start taking notice.

After a couple of brutal pub scenes, the fans started to watch for Bradshaw with anticipation. How many bar patrons could he possibly beat up in one night? Then, when he stepped in the ring, there was a newfound interest—could he dominate a fellow Superstar as easily as he did the drunken locals?

As fun as it is to watch, we all know that drunken locals are much, much, much easier to fight than a WF Superstar.

ACTION	Moves	CONTROL
Facing the Opponent		
Irish Whip to Ropes		●
Fall Away Slam		↓+●
Hard Scoop Slam		←+●
Eye Rake		↑+●
Side Buster		→+●
Chop		✕
Clothesline		↓+✕
Toe Kick		←+✕
Double Axe Handle		↑+✕
Snap Jab		→+✕
Facing the Groggy Opponent		
Jackknife Powerbomb		↓+●
Pendulum Back Breaker		←+●
Rib Breaker		↑+●
DDT		→+●
Behind the Opponent		
Irish Whip to Ropes		●
Pump Handle Drop		↓+●
Back Drop		←+●
Full Nelson Slam		↑+●
Bulldog		→+●
Opponent on Mat		
Upper Body		
Raise Opponent		●
Knee Smash		↑+●
Camel Clutch		→+●
Mounted Punch		←+●
Angry Stomp		✕
Elbow Drop		↓+✕
Angry Stomp		←+✕
Elbow Drop		↑+✕
Angry Stomp		→+✕
Lower Body		
Raise Opponent		●
Boston Crab		↑+●
Leg Lock		→+●
Knee Stomp		←+●
Turnbuckle Moves		
Facing Opponent		
Irish Whip to Ropes		●
Shoulder Thrusts		←+●/→+●
Superplex		↓+●/↑+●
Behind Opponent		
Irish Whip to Ropes		●
Super Back Drop		←+●/→+●
Super Back Drop		↓+●/↑+●
Opponent Sitting in Lower Turnbuckle		
Raise Opponent		●
Foot Choke		←+●/→+●
Foot Choke		↓+●/↑+●
Power Clothesline		▲+✕
Turnbuckle Attacks		
Opponent Standing		
Double Axe Handle		✕
Flying Clothesline		←+✕/→+✕
Flying Clothesline		↓+✕/↑+✕
Opponent on Mat		
Elbow Drop		✕
Knee Drop		←+✕/→+✕
Knee Drop		↓+✕/↑+✕
Running Attacks		
Facing Opponent		
Neckbreaker		●
Spear		←+●/→+●
Spear		↓+●/↑+●
Power Clothesline		✕
Shoulder Block		←+✕/→+✕
Shoulder Block		↓+✕/↑+✕
Behind Opponent		
Bulldog		●
Bulldog		←+●/→+●
Bulldog		↓+●/↑+●
Running Counterattacks—Opponent Running		
Powerslam		←+●/→+●
Powerslam		↓+●/↑+●
Monkey Toss		●

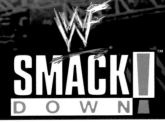

DID YOU KNOW?
Bradshaw is extremely well-educated and very active in the stock market.

Pendulum Back Breaker
←+●
facing a groggy opponent

Rib Breaker
↑+●
in front of groggy opponent

Double Axe Handle
×
from the turnbuckle

Strong Lariat
L1

THE ACOLYTES

Buh-Buh

Height: 6'4"
Weight: 275 lbs.
From: Dudleyville
Favorite Quote: "Thou shalt not mess with the Dudleyz!"
Finishing Move: Dudley Death Drop

BIOGRAPHY

Just about everyone went to school with that one kid who had the unfortunate distinction of being "the kid who talks funny." Regardless of the speech impediment this poor child suffered from, life was very difficult. Not only because of the problem, but also because this kid was usually small, shy, and weak. There was always a bully ready to point out this kid's shortcomings...as if everyone didn't already notice them.

Rather than waste the day hiding in the corner, Buh-Buh Ray probably spent most of his time beating the crap out of anyone stupid enough to pick on him. Maybe it was thanks to having to constantly teach the schoolyard bully that you shouldn't mess with the kid with the speech impediment that Buh-Buh Ray became one of the toughest competitors in all of sports-entertainment.

While competing in another promotion, Buh-Buh Ray solidified his love of extreme fighting and getting a rise out of the crowd with some shocking tactics. Now that he's a Superstar in the World Wrestling Federation, Buh-Buh has got to take those talents and prove he belongs in the big time!

Moves

ACTION	CONTROL
Facing the Opponent	
Irish Whip to Ropes	●
Eye Rake	←+●
Scoop Slam	↑+●
Manhattan Drop	↑+●
Belly to Back Flip	→+●
Body Punch	✕
Clothesline	↓+✕
Toe Kick	←+✕
Double Axe Handle	↑+✕
Overhand Punch	→+✕
Facing the Groggy Opponent	
Piledriver	↓+●
DDT	←+●
Body Press Slam	↑+●
Bearhug	→+●
Behind the Opponent	
Irish Whip to Ropes	●
Back Side Slam	↓+●
Bulldog	←+●
Pumphandle Drop	↑+●
Back Drop	→+●
Opponent on Mat	
Upper Body	
Raise Opponent	●
Sleeper Hold	↑+●
Knee Smash	→+●
Mounted Punch	←+●
Angry Stomp	✕
Elbow Drop	↓+✕
Angry Stomp	←+✕
Elbow Drop	↑+✕
Angry Stomp	→+✕
Lower Body	
Raise Opponent	●
Toss	↑+●
Leg Lock	→+●
Knee Stomp	←+●
Turnbuckle Moves	
Facing Opponent	
Irish Whip to Ropes	●
Choke	←+●/→+●
Superplex	↓+●/↑+●
Behind Opponent	
Irish Whip to Ropes	●
Super Back Drop	←+●/→+●
Super Back Drop	↓+●/↑+●
Opponent Sitting in Lower Turnbuckle	
Raise Opponent	●
Choke	←+●/→+●
Choke	↓+●/↑+●
Clothesline	▲+✕
Turnbuckle Attacks	
Opponent Standing	
Front Dropkick	✕
Double Axe Handle	←+✕/→+✕
Double Axe Handle	↓+✕/↑+✕
Opponent on Mat	
Elbow Drop	✕
Elbow Drop	←+✕/→+✕
Elbow Drop	↓+✕/↑+✕
Running Attacks	
Facing Opponent	
Neckbreaker	●
Neckbreaker	←+●/→+●
Neckbreaker	↓+●/↑+●
Clothesline	✕
Shoulder Block	←+✕/→+✕
Shoulder Block	↓+✕/↑+✕
Behind Opponent	
Bulldog	●
Bulldog	←+●/→+●
Bulldog	↓+●/↑+●
Running Counterattacks—Opponent Running	
Monkey Toss	●
Whirl Sideslam	←+●/→+●
Whirl Sideslam	↓+●/↑+●

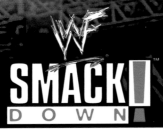

DID YOU KNOW?

Buh-Buh Ray Dudley excelled in the shot-put and discus events while attending St. John's University.

Body Press Sla

↑+●

facing a groggy opponen

Back Side Slam

↓+●

from behind opponent

Neckbreaker

↓+● / ←+● / →+● / ↑+●

running at opponent

Jackknife Powerbomb

L1

THE DUDLEYZ

Chris Jericho

Height: 5'11"
Weight: 225 lbs.
Favorite Quote: "It will never, e...e...e...ever be the same!"
Finishing Move: Walls of Jericho
Career Highlights: Intercontinental Champion

BIOGRAPHY

On August 9, 1999 Chris Jericho made one of the most anticipated debuts in the history of the World Wrestling Federation. After showing his face to an audience watching around the world and receiving a rambunctious ovation from the fans who were live in Chicago, Jericho rambled on and on about how he was the hero the 🅦 so desperately needed. He had no doubt in his mind—"Y2J" was ready to save the day!

The only problem was that the 🅦 definitely *did not* need "Y2J's" help! If Jericho were a baseball player, he would hit the "game-winning" home run when his team was up by six runs. If he were a businessman, he would take over a billion-dollar computer company and promise to bring it back to prosperity.

Perhaps the most amazing thing about "Y2J's" unnecessary call-to-action campaign is that he has the full support of all the Jerichoholics around the world. They know that even though he doesn't need to be playing the role of "super-hero," the "Ayatollah of Rock n' Roll-a" delivers every time he appears on Federation programming or in front of a live audience. If he doesn't deliver with his unparalleled technical ability or high-flying aerial maneuvers, he delivers with his astounding skill on the microphone.

There aren't many Superstars who can talk as much smack as Chris Jericho and have the ability to back it up when the time comes. No matter what his goals for the future are, there is no denying that Chris Jericho truly is a Superstar for the millennium!

Moves

ACTION	CONTROL
Facing the Opponent	
Irish Whip to Ropes	●
DDT	↓+●
Snapmare	←+●
Reverse Suplex	↑+●
Jumping Arm Breaker	→+●
Snap Jab	✕
Clothesline	↓+✕
Middle Kick	←+✕
Spinning Back Kick	↑+✕
Chop	→+✕
Facing the Groggy Opponent	
Jackknife Powerbomb	↓+●
Double Arm Backbreaker	←+●
Fisherman Suplex	↑+●
Small Package	→+●
Behind the Opponent	
Irish Whip to Ropes	●
Reverse Pin	↓+●
Diving Reverse DDT	←+●
Reverse Brainbuster	↑+●
School Boy	→+●
Opponent on Mat	
Upper Body	
Raise Opponent	●
Reverse Chin Lock	↑+●
Knee Smash	→+●
Mounted Punch	←+●
Angry Stomp	✕
Angry Stomp	↓+✕
Austin Elbow Drop	←+✕
Angry Stomp	↑+✕
Austin Elbow Drop	→+✕
Lower Body	
Raise Opponent	●
Toss	↑+●
Kick to Leg	→+●
Walls of Jericho	←+●
Turnbuckle Moves	
Facing Opponent	
Irish Whip to Ropes	●
Mudhole Stomping	←+●/→+●
Superplex	↓+●/↑+●
Behind Opponent	
Irish Whip to Ropes	●
Super Back Drop	←+●/→+●
Super Back Drop	↓+●/↑+●
Opponent Sitting in Lower Turnbuckle	
Raise Opponent	●
Foot Choke	←+●/→+●
Foot Choke	↓+●/↑+●
Back Elbow Attack	▲+✕
Turnbuckle Attacks	
Opponent Standing	
Missile Dropkick	✕
Spinning Wheel Kick	←+✕/→+✕
Spinning Wheel Kick	↓+✕/↑+✕
Opponent on Mat	
Diving Head Butt	✕
Diving Moonsault	←+✕/→+✕
Diving Moonsault	↓+✕/↑+✕
Running Attacks	
Facing Opponent	
Neckbreaker	●
Rolling Clutch Pin	←+●/→+●
Rolling Clutch Pin	↓+●/↑+●
Back Elbow Attack	✕
Shoulder Block	←+✕/→+✕
Shoulder Block	↓+✕/↑+✕
Behind Opponent	
Facecrusher	●
School Boy	←+●/→+●
School Boy	↓+●/↑+●
Running Counterattacks—Opponent Running	
Monkey Toss	●
Shoulder Back Toss	←+●/→+●
Shoulder Back Toss	↓+●/↑+●

30   primagames.com

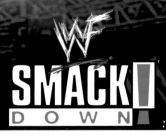

DID YOU KNOW?

Chris Jericho plays in a rock band called "Fozzy Osbourne." Chris Jericho's father, Ted Irvine, played left wing for the New York Rangers.

Reverse Brainbuster
↑+●

from behind opponent

Walls of Jericho
←+●

opponent on mat, lower body

Missile Dropkick
×

from the turnbuckle

Double Powerbomb
L1

CHRIS JERICHO

Christian

Height: 6'
Weight: 215 lbs.
From: Toronto, Ont.
Finishing Move: Crucifix
Career Highlights: Light Heavyweight Champion

BIOGRAPHY

It's easy to forget that Christian has been in the World Wrestling Federation for almost two full years now. And that mysterious aura is only part of what makes him such an amazing Superstar.

He was brought in as the third member of the Brood, and some worried that Christian would get stuck in the shadows because Edge and Gangrel (the other two members of the original Brood) had their own unique qualities that made them stand out to Federation fans and officials. However, it didn't take long for Christian to win over legions of his own fans with his astounding athleticism and silent power.

When problems arose between the other members of the Brood, sides had to be chosen. It didn't take long for Christian to side with his brother, Edge. The young duo decided to be less focused on forcing their Gothic lifestyle on the fans and more focused on success in the ring.

Now dedicated to the tag team scene, Christian quickly established himself as one of the most talented Superstars on the roster. His performance in the unforgettable *No Mercy™ Ladder* Match solidified his future as a major player in the World Wrestling Federation.

Although it seems that singles success is imminent, it would be nice to see Christian join Edge in achieving their childhood dream—winning the World Wrestling Federation Tag-Team Titles together!

ACTION	Moves	CONTROL
Facing the Opponent		
Irish Whip to Ropes		●
Arm Wrench		↓+●
Scoop Slam		←+●
Suplex		↑+●
Side Buster		→+●
Austin Punches		✕
Clothesline		↓+✕
Toe Kick		←+✕
Dropkick		↑+✕
Chop		→+✕
Facing the Groggy Opponent		
Stomach Crusher		↓+●
DDT		←+●
Northern Lights Suplex		↑+●
Sambo Suplex		→+●
Behind the Opponent		
Irish Whip to Ropes		●
Reverse Pin		↓+●
Diving Reverse DDT		←+●
Sleeper Hold		↑+●
German Suplex Pin		→+●
Opponent on Mat		
Upper Body		
Raise Opponent		●
Knee Smash		↑+●
Mounted Punch		→+●
Reverse Chin Lock		←+●
Angry Stomp		✕
Leg Drop		↓+✕
Angry Stomp		←+✕
Leg Drop		↑+✕
Angry Stomp		→+✕
Lower Body		
Raise Opponent		●
Toss		↑+●
Kick to Leg		→+●
Knee Stomp		←+●
Turnbuckle Moves		
Facing Opponent		
Irish Whip to Ropes		●
Mudhole Stomping		←+●/→+●
Foot Choke		↓+●/↑+●
Behind Opponent		
Irish Whip to Ropes		●
Super Back Drop		←+●/→+●
Super Back Drop		↓+●/↑+●
Opponent Sitting in Lower Turnbuckle		
Raise Opponent		●
Foot Choke		←+●/→+●
Foot Choke		↓+●/↑+●
Back Elbow Attack		▲+✕
Turnbuckle Attacks		
Opponent Standing		
Double Axe Handle		✕
Front Dropkick		←+✕/→+✕
Front Dropkick		↓+✕/↑+✕
Opponent on Mat		
Elbow Drop		✕
Knee Drop		←+✕/→+✕
Knee Drop		↓+✕/↑+✕
Running Attacks		
Facing Opponent		
Neckbreaker		●
Spear		←+●/→+●
Spear		↓+●/↑+●
Back Elbow Attack		✕
Clothesline		←+✕/→+✕
Dropkick		↓+✕/↑+✕
Behind Opponent		
School Boy		●
School Boy		←+●/→+●
School Boy		↓+●/↑+●
Running Counterattacks—Opponent Running		
Monkey Toss		●
Shoulder Back Toss		←+●/→+●
Shoulder Back Toss		↓+●/↑+●

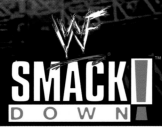

DID YOU KNOW?

Traveling through his home country as a young independent wrestler, Christian misjudged a patch of frozen ice...and fell right through it! Always there to bail ou tag team partner, Edge helped him back to safety.

Dropkick
↑+✕

in front of opponent

German Suplex Pin
→+●

behind the opponent

Foot Choke
↓+●/←+●/→+●/↑+●

opponent in the turnb

Impaler
L1

behind the opponent

Chyna

Finishing Move:
Pedigree
Career Highlights:
Intercontinental
Champion

9TH WONDER OF THE WORLD

BIOGRAPHY

The Grand Canyon, Mount Everest, the Great Barrier Reef and Chyna.

An object earns the title "wonder of the world" because it is something that cannot be duplicated, a sight so awesome that one is often left powerless in its presence. When Chyna first entered the WF, most people could not believe what they were seeing. How could she be so intimidating? Some, very foolishly, cast her off as nothing more than that—an intimidating sight—and they were quickly proven wrong.

Thanks to her incredible physique and technical skill, it is so hard to forget that Chyna is a female. But we have to keep that in mind to truly appreciate what she has been able to do so far in her WF career. She was the first woman to qualify for the *Royal Rumble®*, the first woman to qualify for the *King of the Ring®* tournament, the first female to ever hold a major WF Championship, and a major player in D-Generation X and the Corporation. Forget about this man/woman stuff—anybody would consider themselves lucky to enjoy a career as successful as Chyna's!

What is so great about Chyna is that instead of just complaining about being branded "only a woman," the Ninth Wonder of the World went out and forced everyone to take notice. Destroying any obstacle thrown in her way, Chyna proved to everyone that they had better reevaluate their view on the "battle of the sexes," because if they don't, one day the sexes will battle the hell right out of them.

Moves

ACTION	CONTROL
Facing the Opponent	
Irish Whip to Ropes	●
Club to Neck	↓+●
Snapmare	←+●
Eye Rake	↑+●
Snapmare	→+●
Austin Punches	✕
Clothesline	↓+✕
Chop	←+✕
Double Axe Handle	↑+✕
Toe Kick	→+✕
Facing the Groggy Opponent	
Piledriver	↓+●
Arm Wrench	←+●
Stomach Crusher	↑+●
Rib Breaker	→+●
Behind the Opponent	
Irish Whip to Ropes	●
Low Blow	↓+●
Turn to Face	←+●
Low Blow	↑+●
Turn to Face	→+●
Opponent on Mat	
Upper Body	
Raise Opponent	●
Mounted Punch	↑+●
Mounted Punch	→+●
Mounted Punch	←+●
Angry Stomp	✕
Elbow Drop	↓+✕
Angry Stomp	←+✕
Elbow Drop	↑+✕
Angry Stomp	→+✕
Lower Body	
Raise Opponent	●
Knee Stomp	↑+●
Kick to Groin	→+●
Kick to Groin	←+●
Turnbuckle Moves	
Facing Opponent	
Irish Whip to Ropes	●
Shoulder Thrusts	←+●/→+●
Choke	↓+●/↑+●
Behind Opponent	
Irish Whip to Ropes	●
Low Blow	←+●/→+●
Low Blow	↓+●/↑+●
Opponent Sitting in Lower Turnbuckle	
Raise Opponent	●
Foot Choke	←+●/→+●
Foot Choke	↓+●/↑+●
Shoulder Block	▲+✕
Turnbuckle Attacks	
Opponent Standing	
Double Axe Handle	✕
Double Axe Handle	←+✕/→+✕
Double Axe Handle	↓+✕/↑+✕
Opponent on Mat	
Elbow Drop	✕
Elbow Drop	←+✕/→+✕
Elbow Drop	↓+✕/↑+✕
Running Attacks	
Facing Opponent	
Spear	●
Spear	←+●/→+●
Spear	↓+●/↑+●
Shoulder Block	✕
Thump	←+✕/→+✕
Thump	↓+✕/↑+✕
Behind Opponent	
School Boy	●
School Boy	←+●/→+●
School Boy	↓+●/→+●
Running Counterattacks—Opponent Running	
Monkey Toss	●
Powerslam	←+●/→+●
Powerslam	↓+●/↑+●

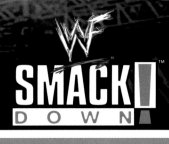

SMACK! DOWN!

Prima's Official Strategy G

DID YOU KNOW?

Chyna graduated from the University of Tampa with 2 degrees: Spanish and Liter

Low Blow
↓+●/↑+●
opponent on groun

Elbow Drop
↓+×
opponent on ground

Mounted Pu
↑+●/←+●/→+●
opponent on grou

Pedigree
L1

Chyna

primagames.com

Debra

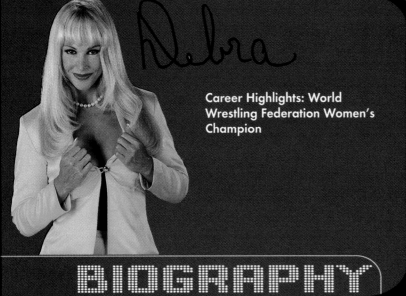

Debra (signature)

Career Highlights: World Wrestling Federation Women's Champion

BIOGRAPHY

When the time comes to look back on Debra's career in the WWF, there is no doubt that we will point to *Rock Bottom™* (the December 1998 Pay-Per-View) as a monumental event. That was the night she figured out what was going to send her straight to the top, and fast. As Debra started to pay up on a bet and take off her clothes, the sold-out arena went ballistic.

During these intense moments, the thousands of male fans in attendance were on their feet and ready to obey Debra's every whim. And if the fans were hypnotized by her incomparable figure, why wouldn't the rest of the male-dominated World Wrestling Federation be?

Although Debra never completed the action that night, she learned a valuable lesson: showing off her body would get her exactly what she was after—everything!

The most ingenious part of Debra's master strategy was that she tried her hardest to never appear to be more than a body. You never heard her utter anything such as, "I want people to see past my looks and find out who I really am," or "Behind my exterior is a fascinating and intelligent women."

The fact of the matter is that Debra is really, really hot and most guys would hand her the world even if she wore oversized T-shirts and sweat pants.

But aren't we all extremely lucky that Debra doesn't want to take that chance?

ACTION	Moves	CONTROL
Facing the Opponent		
Irish Whip to Ropes		●
Club to Neck		↓+●
Snapmare		←+●
Arm Wrench		↑+●
Snapmare		→+●
Slap		✕
Middle Kick		↓+✕
Toe Kick		←+✕
Double Axe Handle		↑+✕
Chop		→+✕
Facing the Groggy Opponent		
Suplex		↓+●
Snapmare		←+●
Arm Wrench		↑+●
Snapmare		→+●
Behind the Opponent		
Irish Whip to Ropes		●
Reverse Pin		↓+●
Turn to Face		←+●
Reverse Pin		↑+●
Turn to Face		→+●
Opponent on Mat		
Upper Body		
Raise Opponent		●
Sleeper Hold		↑+●
Knee Smash		→+●
Knee Smash		←+●
Angry Stomp		✕
Angry Stomp		↓+✕
Angry Stomp		←+✕
Angry Stomp		↑+✕
Angry Stomp		→+✕
Lower Body		
Raise Opponent		●
Knee Stomp		↑+●
Leg Lock		→+●
Leg Lock		←+●
Turnbuckle Moves		
Facing Opponent		
Irish Whip to Ropes		●
Choke		←+●/→+●
Shoulder Thrusts		↓+●/↑+●
Behind Opponent		
Irish Whip to Ropes		●
School Boy		←+●/→+●
School Boy		↓+●/↑+●
Opponent Sitting in Lower Turnbuckle		
Raise Opponent		●
Choke		←+●/→+●
Choke		↓+●/↑+●
Shoulder Block		▲+✕
Turnbuckle Attacks		
Opponent Standing		
Double Axe Handle		✕
Double Axe Handle		←+✕/→+✕
Double Axe Handle		↓+✕/↑+✕
Opponent on Mat		
Knee Drop		✕
Knee Drop		←+✕/→+✕
Knee Drop		↓+✕/↑+✕
Running Attacks		
Facing Opponent		
Neckbreaker		●
Neckbreaker		←+●/→+●
Neckbreaker		↓+●/↑+●
Shoulder Block		✕
Shoulder Block		←+✕/→+✕
Shoulder Block		↓+✕/↑+✕
Behind Opponent		
Bulldog		●
Bulldog		←+●/→+●
Bulldog		↓+●/↑+●
Running Counterattacks—Opponent Running		
Monkey Toss		●
Shoulder Back Toss		←+●/→+●
Shoulder Back Toss		↓+●/↑+●

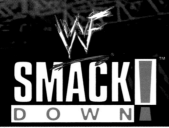
DID YOU KNOW?

Debra helped a couple of friends raise money to save homeless puppies.

Double Axe Handle
↑+✕
in front of opponent

Shoulder Thrusts
↓+● / ↑+●
opponent in turnbuckle

Club to Neck
↓+●
in front of opponent

DDT
L1

D'Lo Brown

Height: 6'3"
Weight: 268 lbs.
From: Chicago, IL
Favorite Quote: "You better recognize!"
Finishing Move: 'Lo Down
Career Highlights:
European Champion
Intercontinental Champion

BIOGRAPHY

If you ask any World Wrestling Federation fan or official to name the five Superstars who will have the biggest impact in the next few years, there is no doubt that D'Lo Brown would appear on each of those lists. An intelligent and articulate young man, D'Lo possesses the athletic ability that most people dream about.

With the Sky High and the 'Lo Down, D'Lo gets the action going above the canvas...but he's more than willing to show off his technical prowess and grind it out on the mat. You can liken his overall abilities to the "bobble head" that he has made famous on his walks down to the ring. You're never sure where it's going next, and you're transfixed at the mere sight of it.

A former certified public accountant, there is little question that D'Lo has the brains to propel him to the next level. Using the precise preparation tactics that C.P.A.s are infamous for, D'Lo never enters a contest without a detailed strategy.

Everyone knows what D'Lo achieved while serving as the European Champion, but what remains to be seen is whether or not he can put all his tools and talents together to become as dominating a Superstar as everyone expects.

Moves

ACTION	CONTROL
Facing the Opponent	
Irish Whip to Ropes	●
Piledriver	↓+●
Hard Scoop Slam	←+●
Suplex	↑+●
Side Buster	→+●
Snap Jab	✕
Jumping Calf Kick	↓+✕
Austin Punches	←+✕
Double Axe Handle	↑+✕
Shuffle Side Kick	→+✕
Facing the Groggy Opponent	
Running Powerbomb	↓+●
Whirl Side Slam	←+●
Sky High	↑+●
Pendulum Backbreaker	→+●
Behind the Opponent	
Irish Whip to Ropes	●
Atomic Drop	↓+●
Back Drop	←+●
Sleeper Hold	↑+●
School Boy	→+●
Opponent on Mat	
Upper Body	
Raise Opponent	●
Knee Smash	↑+●
Mounted Punch	→+●
Sleeper Hold	←+●
Angry Stomp	✕
Angry Stomp	↓+✕
D'Lo Leg Drop	←+✕
Angry Stomp	↑+✕
D'Lo Leg Drop	→+✕
Lower Body	
Raise Opponent	●
Leg Lock	↑+●
Kick to Leg	→+●
D'Lo Texas Cloverleaf	←+●
Turnbuckle Moves	
Facing Opponent	
Irish Whip to Ropes	●
Frankensteiner	←+●/→+●
Shoulder Thrust	↓+●/↑+●
Behind Opponent	
Irish Whip to Ropes	●
Super Back Drop	←+●/→+●
Super Back Drop	↓+●/↑+●
Opponent Sitting in Lower Turnbuckle	
Raise Opponent	●
Foot Choke	←+●/→+●
Foot Choke	↓+●/↑+●
Shoulder Block	▲+✕
Turnbuckle Attacks	
Opponent Standing	
Spinning Wheel Kick	✕
Front Dropkick	←+✕/→+✕
Front Dropkick	↓+✕/↑+✕
Opponent on Mat	
Twisting Body Attack	✕
Knee Drop	←+✕/→+✕
Knee Drop	↓+✕/↑+✕
Running Attacks	
Facing Opponent	
Neckbreaker Drop	●
Rolling Clutch Pin	←+●/→+●
Rolling Clutch Pin	↓+●/↑+●
Dropkick	✕
Clothesline	←+✕/→+✕
Clothesline	↓+✕/↑+✕
Behind Opponent	
School Boy	●
School Boy	←+●/→+●
School Boy	↓+●/↑+●
Running Counterattacks—Opponent Running	
Monkey Toss	●
Pulling Walk Slam	←+●/→+●
Pulling Walk Slam	↓+●/↑+●

DID YOU KNOW?

Before coming into the WWF, D'Lo struggled with his weight, ballooning up to 400 lbs. at one time. Crediting hard work, determination and support from his loved ones, he shed it to become the agile superstar he is today.

Sky High

↑ + ●

facing the
groggy opponent

Whirl Side Slam

← + ●

in front of
groggy opponent

D'Lo Leg Drop

← + X

opponent on mat, upper body

The 'Lo Down

L1

D'LŌ™ BROWN

D-Von Dudley

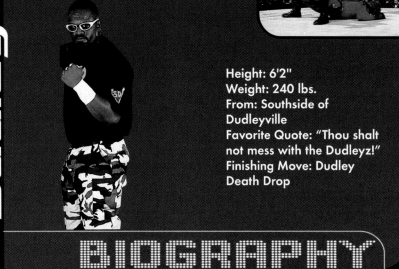

Height: 6'2"
Weight: 240 lbs.
From: Southside of Dudleyville
Favorite Quote: "Thou shalt not mess with the Dudleyz!"
Finishing Move: Dudley Death Drop

BIOGRAPHY

Throughout the entire sports-entertainment world, the Dudley Boyz have a reputation for being two of the toughest competitors. And D-Von does more than his fair share to keep up the hype!

Before arriving in the World Wrestling Federation, the Dudley Boyz honed their skills in the extreme arena. Known for a stiff offense and even stiffer language, the Dudley Boyz earned a lot of respect from their peers at the time.

However, they had to prove themselves in the "big time." Having to leave some of their old tactics behind, D-Von and Buh-Buh Ray brought their unique style of sports-entertainment over to the WF and quickly earned the respect they had in other arenas. Although there is nothing funny about them, D-Von is quick to dispel any laughter that his tag team partner may have stirred up among the fans.

After Buh-Buh is able to get out whatever it is he's trying to say, D-Von is quick to jump in and take the hard-line with their opponents.

D-Von wants everyone to know that "Thou shalt not mess with the Dudleyz!"

Moves

ACTION	CONTROL
Facing the Opponent	
Irish Whip to Ropes	●
DDT	↓+●
Snapmare	←+●
Suplex	↑+●
Club to Neck	→+●
Austin Punches	✕
Shuffle Side Kick	↓+✕
Chop	←+✕
Double Axe Handle	↑+✕
Toe Kick	→+✕
Facing the Groggy Opponent	
Piledriver	↓+●
Fall Away Slam	←+●
Manhattan Drop	↑+●
Pendulum Backbreaker	→+●
Behind the Opponent	
Irish Whip to Ropes	●
Atomic Drop	↓+●
Back Drop	←+●
Diving Reverse DDT	↑+●
Bulldog	→+●
Opponent on Mat	
Upper Body	
Raise Opponent	●
Camel Clutch	↑+●
Mounted Punch	→+●
Knee Smash	←+●
Angry Stomp	✕
Leg Drop	↓+✕
Angry Stomp	←+✕
Leg Drop	↑+✕
Angry Stomp	→+✕
Lower Body	
Raise Opponent	●
Toss	↑+●
Kick to Leg	→+●
Knee Stomp	←+●
Turnbuckle Moves	
Facing Opponent	
Irish Whip to Ropes	●
Foot Choke	←+●/→+●
Superplex	↓+●/↑+●
Behind Opponent	
Irish Whip to Ropes	●
Super Back Drop	←+●/→+●
Super Back Drop	↓+●/↑+●
Opponent Sitting in Lower Turnbuckle	
Raise Opponent	●
Choke	←+●/→+●
Choke	↓+●/↑+●
Clothesline	▲+✕
Turnbuckle Attacks	
Opponent Standing	
Double Axe Handle	✕
Double Axe Handle	←+✕/→+✕
Double Axe Handle	↓+✕/↑+✕
Opponent on Mat	
Elbow Drop	✕
Diving Head Butt	←+✕/→+✕
Diving Head Butt	↓+✕/↑+✕
Running Attacks	
Facing Opponent	
Neckbreaker	●
Neckbreaker	←+●/→+●
Neckbreaker	↓+●/↑+●
Clothesline	✕
Diving Shoulder	←+✕/→+✕
Diving Shoulder	↓+✕/↑+✕
Behind Opponent	
School Boy	●
School Boy	←+●/→+●
School Boy	↓+●/↑+●
Running Counterattacks—Opponent Running	
Monkey Toss	●
Shoulder Back Toss	←+●/→+●
Shoulder Back Toss	↓+●/↑+●

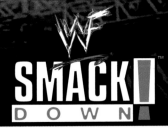

DID YOU KNOW?

As legend has it, D-Von was born after his father, Big Daddy Dudley (a man known for his numerous "encounters") got stranded in the South Side of Dudleyville.

Diving Reverse DDT

↑+●

behind an opponent

Back Drop

←+●

behind an opponent

 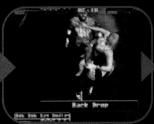 

Snapmore

←+●

in front of opponent

Jackknife Powerbomb

L1

THE DUDLEYZ

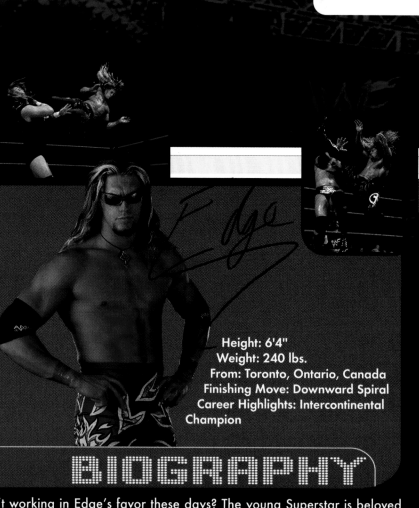

Edge

Height: 6'4"
Weight: 240 lbs.
From: Toronto, Ontario, Canada
Finishing Move: Downward Spiral
Career Highlights: Intercontinental Champion

BIOGRAPHY

What isn't working in Edge's favor these days? The young Superstar is beloved by every type of World Wrestling Federation fan, and his ability in the ring is recognized as among the best.

One of the more amazing things about Edge is his broad appeal. At sold-out arenas all over the world, women scream for his long blond locks and larger-than-life smile. They are drawn in by his strong presence that demands attention, even though he never asks for it.

Men are into Edge because of the coolness factor. The sunglasses, long trench coat, great theme song, and uncanny entrance all add to this. Plus, Edge has a dark side to him that is sadistic and uncontrollable. It is an aspect of human nature that many men have, but few are brave (or insane) enough to ever let surface. Men everywhere can live that side of their souls vicariously through Edge.

During a number of singles matches over the past few months, and especially while competing in the *Terri Invitational at No Mercy*™, Edge had the opportunity to display the skill in the ring that has most Federation officials salivating at the thought of his future in the industry.

With a wave of momentum like this, is there anyone or anything that can stop Edge from reaching the top?

Moves

ACTION	CONTROL
Facing the Opponent	
Irish Whip to Ropes	●
Scissors Sweep	↓+●
Snapmare	←+●
Reverse Suplex	↑+●
Scoop Slam	→+●
Snap Jab	✕
Dropkick	↓+✕
Chop	←+✕
Shuffle Side Kick	↑+✕
Elbow Smash	→+✕
Facing the Groggy Opponent	
DDT	↓+●
Spinning Back Drop	←+●
Stomach Crusher	↑+●
Rib Breaker	→+●
Behind the Opponent	
Irish Whip to Ropes	●
Full Nelson Slam	↓+●
Back Side Slam	←+●
Electric Chair Drop	↑+●
Face Crusher	→+●
Opponent on Mat	
Upper Body	
Raise Opponent	●
Knee Smash	↑+●
Short Arm Scissors	→+●
Mounted Punch	←+●
Angry Stomp	✕
Leg Drop	↓+✕
Angry Stomp	←+✕
Leg Drop	↑+✕
Angry Stomp	→+✕
Lower Body	
Raise Opponent	●
Toss	↑+●
Knee Stomp	→+●
Leg Lock	←+●
Turnbuckle Moves	
Facing Opponent	
Irish Whip to Ropes	●
Shoulder Thrust	←+●/→+●
Frankensteiner	↓+●/↑+●
Behind Opponent	
Irish Whip to Ropes	●
Super Back Drop	←+●/→+●
Super Back Drop	↓+●/↑+●
Opponent Sitting in Lower Turnbuckle	
Raise Opponent	●
Choke	←+●/→+●
Choke	↓+●/↑+●
Shoulder Block	▲+✕
Turnbuckle Attacks	
Opponent Standing	
Missile Dropkick	✕
Diving Spear	←+✕/→+✕
Diving Spear	↓+✕/↑+✕
Opponent on Mat	
Knee Drop	✕
Knee Drop	←+✕/→+✕
Knee Drop	↓+✕/↑+✕
Running Attacks	
Facing Opponent	
Spear	●
Spear	←+●/→+●
Spear	↓+●/↑+●
Spinning Wheel Kick	✕
Dropkick	←+✕/→+✕
Dropkick	↓+✕/↑+✕
Behind Opponent	
Facecrusher	●
School Boy	←+●/→+●
School Boy	↓+●/↑+●

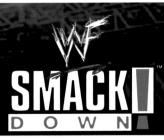

DID YOU KNOW?

Edge proposed to Val Venis' sister while on the 1999 *Wrestle Vessel*.

Spinning Back Drop
←+●
in front of groggy opponent

Reverse Suplex
↑+●
in front of opponent

Back Side Slam
←+●
behind opponent

Downward Spiral
L1

Faarooq

Faarooq (signature)

Height: 6'7"
Weight: 270 lbs.
Finishing Move: Dominator
Career Highlights: Tag Team Champion

BIOGRAPHY

Most finishing maneuvers in the World Wrestling Federation are given names that reflect their characters' personality. The names must also be intimidating and catchy. The Pedigree, the Rock Bottom, and the Showstopper Chokeslam all meet these criteria. But there is perhaps no name throughout the industry more fitting than Faarooq's "Dominator."

"Dominator"—the move—describes Faarooq's modified powerbomb that drops his opponents face first on the canvas. "Dominator"—the man—describes the Superstar performing the move.

Ever since being an all-American stud at Florida State, Ron Simmons has been used to dominating his environment and the competition that surrounds it. When Ron made the transition to sports-entertainment, he found that dominating opponents in the squared circle came just as naturally to him as destroying them on the gridiron.

There is no doubt that Faarooq achieved a great deal of success in the early days of his career, but as a member of the Acolytes, he has really elevated his game to an all-time high.

Emerging out of the Ministry of Darkness, Faarooq and Bradshaw have both made the most of the opportunity that the Acolytes have provided. Spending his time on screen much the same way he spends his time off it (drinking beer and kicking @#$), Faarooq is not only enjoying his latest achievements in the ring, but he's having a great time doing it!

Moves

ACTION	CONTROL
Facing the Opponent	
Irish Whip to Ropes	●
Bearhug Front Slam	↓+●
Hard Scoop Slam	←+●
Rib Breaker	↑+●
DDT	→+●
Austin Punches	✕
Clothesline	↓+✕
Toe Kick	←+✕
Double Axe Handle	↑+✕
Chop	→+✕
Facing the Groggy Opponent	
Jackknife Powerbomb	↓+●
Rib Breaker	←+●
Body Press Slam	↑+●
Spinebuster	→+●
Behind the Opponent	
Irish Whip to Ropes	●
Atomic Drop	↓+●
Back Drop	←+●
Full Nelson Slam	↑+●
Abdominal Stretch	→+●
Opponent on Mat	
Upper Body	
Raise Opponent	●
Camel Clutch	↑+●
Sleeper Hold	→+●
Mounted Punch	←+●
Angry Stomp	✕
Elbow Drop	↓+✕
Angry Stomp	←+✕
Elbow Drop	↑+✕
Angry Stomp	→+✕
Lower Body	
Raise Opponent	●
Boston Crab	↑+●
Kick to Groin	→+●
Knee Stomp	←+●
Turnbuckle Moves	
Facing Opponent	
Irish Whip to Ropes	●
Shoulder Thrusts	←+●/→+●
Choke	↓+●/↑+●
Behind Opponent	
Irish Whip to Ropes	●
Super Back Drop	←+●/→+●
Super Back Drop	↓+●/↑+●
Opponent Sitting in Lower Turnbuckle	
Raise Opponent	●
Foot Choke	←+●/→+●
Foot Choke	↓+●/↑+●
Clothesline	▲+✕
Turnbuckle Attacks	
Opponent Standing	
Double Axe Handle	✕
Flying Clothesline	←+✕/→+✕
Flying Clothesline	↓+✕/↑+✕
Opponent on Mat	
Diving Head Butt	✕
Knee Drop	←+✕/→+✕
Knee Drop	↓+✕/↑+✕
Running Attacks	
Facing Opponent	
Neckbreaker	●
Spear	←+●/→+●
Spear	↓+●/↑+●
Clothesline	✕
Diving Shoulder	←+✕/→+✕
Diving Shoulder	↓+✕/↑+✕
Behind Opponent	
Bulldog	●
Bulldog	←+●/→+●
Bulldog	↓+●/↑+●
Running Counterattacks—Opponent Running	
Powerslam	●
Spinebuster	←+●/→+●
Spinebuster	↓+●/↑+●

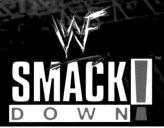

DID YOU KNOW?

Faarooq was an all-American football stud at Florida State University before sta
his career in sports-entertainment.

Camel Clutch
↑+●
opponent on the ground

Bearhug Front Slam
↓+●
in front of opponent

Full Nelson S
↑+●
from behind oppon

Dominator
L1

Gangrel*

Height: 6'0"
Weight: 234 lbs.
Finishing Move: Impaler

BIOGRAPHY

Show me a man who rises through a ring of fire on his way to the ring, has fangs instead of teeth and spits out a mysterious, red viscous liquid, before his matches, and I'll show you someone with a long future as a World Wrestling Federation Superstar!

Gangrel encompasses all that the World Wrestling Federation has come to stand for over the past couple of years. He has an entrance unlike any other, and you're just as excited to see Gangrel make his way to the ring as you are to see him finish off his opponent with a devastating Impaler DDT.

Capitalizing on the "Goth" culture that is all the rage with young adults across the country, Gangrel is the consummate showman who has attracted a varied fan base. Teenage girls dressed all in black, guys who like it hardcore, and grandmas who like to remain young at heart have their own reasons for being on Gangrel's side.

Already logging time with Edge, Christian, and the Hardy Boyz, Gangrel has been associated with some of the best young talent the Federation has to offer. If it was his backstage wisdom that helped propel these four Superstars along, you'd have to believe it will not be long before Gangrel has a couple of pals rising up through the stage with him again.

ACTION	Moves	CONTROL
Facing the Opponent		
Irish Whip to Ropes		●
Manhattan Drop		↓+●
Gangrel Suplex		←+●
Eye Rake		↑+●
DDT		→+●
Chop		✕
Clothesline		↓+✕
Toe Kick		←+✕
Shuffle Side Kick		↑+✕
Body Punch		→+✕
Facing the Groggy Opponent		
Piledriver		↓+●
Gangrel Suplex		←+●
Headlock and Punch		↑+●
Manhattan Drop		→+●
Behind the Opponent		
Irish Whip to Ropes		●
Pumphandle Slam		↓+●
Back Drop		←+●
Sleeper Hold		↑+●
Diving Reverse DDT		→+●
Opponent on Mat		
Upper Body		
Raise Opponent		●
Knee Smash		↑+●
Mounted Punch		→+●
Sleeper Hold		←+●
Angry Stomp		✕
Elbow Drop		↓+✕
Double Knee Drop		←+✕
Elbow Drop		↑+✕
Double Knee Drop		→+✕
Lower Body		
Raise Opponent		●
Kick to Groin		↑+●
Toss		→+●
Knee Stomp		←+●
Turnbuckle Moves		
Facing Opponent		
Irish Whip to Ropes		●
Mudhole Stomping		←+●/→+●
Tornado DDT		↓+●/↑+●
Behind Opponent		
Irish Whip to Ropes		●
Super Back Drop		←+●/→+●
Super Back Drop		↓+●/↑+●
Opponent Sitting in Lower Turnbuckle		
Raise Opponent		●
Choke		←+●/→+●
Choke		↓+●/↑+●
Back Elbow Attack		▲+✕
Turnbuckle Attacks		
Opponent Standing		
Double Axe Handle		✕
Flying Clothesline		←+✕/→+✕
Flying Clothesline		↓+✕/↑+✕
Opponent on Mat		
Elbow Drop		✕
Knee Drop		←+✕/→+✕
Knee Drop		↓+✕/↑+✕
Running Attacks		
Facing Opponent		
Neckbreaker		●
Neckbreaker Drop		←+●/→+●
Neckbreaker Drop		↓+●/↑+●
Back Elbow Attack		✕
Clothesline		←+✕/→+✕
Clothesline		↓+✕/↑+✕
Behind Opponent		
School Boy		●
School Boy		←+●/→+●
School Boy		↓+●/↑+●

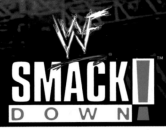
DID YOU KNOW?

This should come as no surprise, but Gangrel and his wife, Luna, officially tied the knot on Halloween in 1994.

Gangrel Suplex

←+●

in front of opponent

Power Slam

↓+●/←+●/→+●/↑+●

opponent running at you

Flying Clothesline

↓+✕/←+✕/→+✕/↑+✕

standing on the turnbuckle

Inverted DDT

L1

GANGREL

The Godfather

Height: 6'6"
Weight: 320 lbs.
From: Red Light District
Favorite Quote: "Pimpin' Ain't Easy!"
Finishing Move: Pimp Drop
Career Highlights: Intercontinental Champion

BIOGRAPHY

Although it ain't easy, he knows he ain't the only one up in this joint!

We're fairly certain that the Godfather isn't saying that there are business competitors of his out in the audience, but that he's confident that there are other people present who enjoy having a good time in the company of some fine lookin' hos!

The most amazing thing about the Godfather is that he's able to concentrate during his matches. Knowing that there are a handful of hotties outside the ring waiting to jump on him the minute the match ends, it's a wonder the Godfather doesn't look to finish all his matches in less time than it would take an 18-year-old to...well, let's just say we're surprised he doesn't try to finish as fast as he can.

We don't know about you, but the Ho Train sounds like something we want to get hit with as much as possible. With the 330-pound Godfather as the conductor though, it doesn't sound as much fun as it should be.

From the outside looking in, it appears that the Godfather is always having a good time, but it might be smart to stay out of his way if you can. After all, he can't relieve *all* his tension with the hos!

ACTION	Moves	CONTROL
Facing the Opponent		
Irish Whip to Ropes		●
Manhattan Drop		↓+●
Hard Scoop Slam		←+●
Club to Neck		↑+●
Suplex		→+●
Austin Punches		✕
Shuffle Side Kick		↓+✕
Chop		←+✕
Clothesline		↑+✕
Overhand Punch		→+✕
Facing the Groggy Opponent		
Piledriver		↓+●
Pendulum Backbreaker		←+●
Headlock and Punch		↑+●
Fall Away Slam		→+●
Behind the Opponent		
Irish Whip to Ropes		●
Atomic Drop		↓+●
Russian Leg Sweep		←+●
Diving Reverse DDT		↑+●
Bulldog		→+●
Opponent on Mat		
Upper Body		
Raise Opponent		●
Short Arm Scissors		↑+●
Sleeper Hold		→+●
Camel Clutch		←+●
Angry Stomp		✕
Elbow Drop		↓+✕
Leg Drop		←+✕
Elbow Drop		↑+✕
Leg Drop		→+✕
Lower Body		
Raise Opponent		●
Leg Lock		↑+●
Kick to Leg		→+●
Knee Stomp		←+●
Turnbuckle Moves		
Facing Opponent		
Irish Whip to Ropes		●
Shoulder Thrusts		←+●/→+●
10 Punch		↓+●/↑+●
Behind Opponent		
Irish Whip to Ropes		●
Super Back Drop		←+●/→+●
Super Back Drop		↓+●/↑+●
Opponent Sitting in Lower Turnbuckle		
Raise Opponent		●
Foot Choke		←+●/→+●
Foot Choke		↓+●/↑+●
Ho Train Attack		▲+✕
Turnbuckle Attacks		
Opponent Standing		
Double Axe Handle		✕
Shoulder Block		←+✕/→+✕
Shoulder Block		↓+✕/↑+✕
Opponent on Mat		
Elbow Drop		✕
Elbow Drop		←+✕/→+✕
Elbow Drop		↓+✕/↑+✕
Running Attacks		
Facing Opponent		
Neckbreaker		●
Rolling Clutch Pin		←+●/→+●
Rolling Clutch Pin		↓+●/↑+●
Diving Shoulder		✕
Ho Train Attack		←+✕/→+✕
Ho Train Attack		↓+✕/↑+✕
Behind Opponent		
School Boy		●
School Boy		←+●/→+●
School Boy		↓+●/↑+●
Running Counterattacks—Opponent Running		
Monkey Toss		●
Samoan Drop		←+●/→+●
Samoan Drop		↓+●/↑+●

DID YOU KNOW?
When the Godfather is home in Las Vegas, one of his favorite activities is designing tattoos.

Manhattan Drop
↓+●

in front of opponent

Russian Leg Sweep
←+●

behind the opponent

Ho Train Attack
↓+●/←+●/→+●/↑+●

running at opponent

Pimp Drop
L1

Godfather
PIMPIN' AIN'T EASY!

Hardcore Holly

Height: 6'6"
Weight: 400 lbs.
From: Mobile, AL
Favorite Quote:
"Hey...Big Shot!"
Career Highlights:
Hardcore Champion,
Tag Team Champion

BIOGRAPHY

For years Bob Holly struggled to find his niche in the World Wrestling Federation. Handed unsuccessful gimmicks and less-than-stellar story lines, the Alabama native was locked in a mid-carders' prison—mediocrity.

This wouldn't have bothered a lesser man, but Holly knew that he was capable of much bigger and better things. So when the time came to put up or shut up, he decided to throw out the rule book and earn his respect the hard way—in the Hardcore Division!

Using anger as his fuel, Holly put on some of the most astonishing contests the division had ever seen. After earning everyone's respect with an unbelievable victory over Al Snow in the Mississippi River, Hardcore Holly was ready to move up the Federation ladder. And what better way to do this than aim for the top and work your way down?

Showing an incredible tolerance for punishment, Hardcore made a weekly habit of strutting to the ring and calling out any big shot who met his minimum height and weight requirements. These strict rules usually left everyone out except Superstars such as Kane, Big Show, The Undertaker and Vis.

He might not have always beaten these giants, but Hardcore Holly certainly learned some valuable lessons. Now, whenever this super heavyweight steps in the ring, his opponents and fans all know that you'd better be a big shot if you want to measure up to Hardcore Holly.

Moves

ACTION	CONTROL
Facing the Opponent	
Irish Whip to Ropes	●
Club to Neck	↓+●
Snapmare	←+●
Arm Wrench	↑+●
Scoop Slam	→+●
Austin Punches	✕
Clothesline	↓+✕
Chop	←+✕
Double Axe Handle	↑+✕
Toe Kick	→+✕
Facing the Groggy Opponent	
Jackknife Powerbomb	↓+●
DDT	←+●
Piledriver	↑+●
Manhattan Drop	→+●
Behind the Opponent	
Irish Whip to Ropes	●
Atomic Drop	↓+●
Back Drop	←+●
Diving Reverse DDT	↑+●
Bulldog	→+●
Opponent on Mat	
Upper Body	
Raise Opponent	●
Sleeper Hold	↑+●
Knee Smash	→+●
Mounted Punch	←+●
Angry Stomp	✕
Double Knee Drop	↓+✕
Angry Stomp	←+✕
Double Knee Drop	↑+✕
Angry Stomp	→+✕
Lower Body	
Raise Opponent	●
Toss	↑+●
Kick to Leg	→+●
Knee Stomp	←+●
Turnbuckle Moves	
Facing Opponent	
Irish Whip to Ropes	●
Frankensteiner	←+●/→+●
Shoulder Thrusts	↓+●/↑+●
Behind Opponent	
Irish Whip to Ropes	●
Super Back Drop	←+●/→+●
Super Back Drop	↓+●/↑+●
Opponent Sitting in Lower Turnbuckle	
Raise Opponent	●
Choke	←+●/→+●
Choke	↓+●/↑+●
Shoulder Block	▲+✕
Turnbuckle Attacks	
Opponent Standing	
Double Axe Handle	✕
Front Dropkick	←+✕/→+✕
Front Dropkick	↓+✕/↑+✕
Opponent on Mat	
Elbow Drop	✕
Knee Drop	←+✕/→+✕
Knee Drop	↓+✕/↑+✕
Running Attacks	
Facing Opponent	
Neckbreaker	●
Spear	←+●/→+●
Spear	↓+●/↑+●
Dropkick	✕
Shoulder Block	←+✕/→+✕
Shoulder Block	↓+✕/↑+✕
Behind Opponent	
Bulldog	●
Bulldog	←+●/→+●
Bulldog	↓+●/↑+●
Running Counterattacks—Opponent Running	
Monkey Toss	●
Powerslam	←+●/→+●
Powerslam	↓+●/↑+●

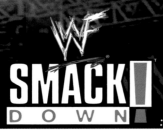

DID YOU KNOW?
When WWF.com's **Byte This** first started, Hardcore Holly was featured in a segment called "Bitter Bob."

Jackknife Powerbomb
↓+●

in front of a groggy oppo

Frankensteiner
←+●/→+●

opponent in turnbuckle

Bulldog
●

running at an oppon
from behind

Falcon Arrow
L1

Hardcore HOLLY™

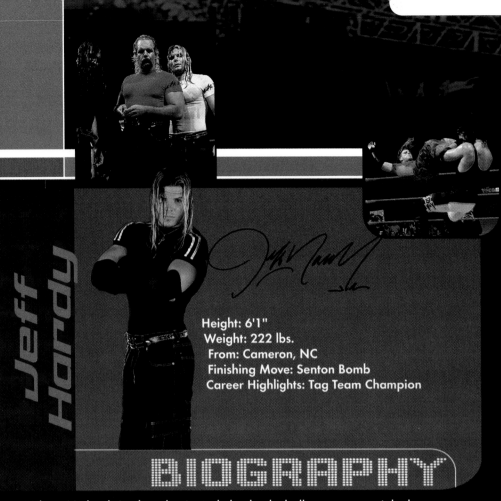

Jeff Hardy

Height: 6'1"
Weight: 222 lbs.
From: Cameron, NC
Finishing Move: Senton Bomb
Career Highlights: Tag Team Champion

BIOGRAPHY

When Michael Jordan dominated the basketball court, one sight became very familiar in arenas throughout the country. Every time "his Airness" got the ball in his hands, tens of thousands of fans got their cameras ready. There was a very good chance that they were about to witness history. You never knew what to expect from number 23, and you always had to be ready to capture the moment forever.

This thinking also applies to Jeff Hardy when he's in competition. Will it be a "Senton Bomb" from the top rope or some other indescribable flying maneuver? It doesn't matter which he chooses, you'd better have that camera in front of your face and your finger on the button.

Some days it seems that Jeff is more an "aerial artist" than he is a "grappler." Attempting—and pulling off—moves that 99% of the athletes in this business don't even dream about, the younger Hardy is always ready to leave a crowd with their jaws on the floor.

Of all he is able to pull off in and around the squared circle, the scariest thing about Jeff Hardy is how far he may be able to go in his career as a Superstar. Barely old enough to legally consume alcohol, Jeff has already worn Federation gold and competed in one of the greatest matches in history.

Moves

ACTION	CONTROL
Facing the Opponent	
Irish Whip to Ropes	●
Arm Wrench	↓+●
Snapmare	←+●
Suplex	↑+●
Scoop Slam	→+●
Chop	✕
Dropkick	↓+✕
Snap Jab	←+✕
Shuffle Side Kick	↑+✕
Austin Punches	→+✕
Facing the Groggy Opponent	
Knee Smash	↓+●
DDT	←+●
Hurracanrana	↑+●
Gangrel Suplex	→+●
Behind the Opponent	
Irish Whip to Ropes	●
Diving Reverse DDT	↓+●
Back Drop	←+●
Back Side Slam	↑+●
German Suplex Slam	→+●
Opponent on Mat	
Upper Body	
Raise Opponent	●
Knee Smash	↑+●
Sleeper Hold	→+●
Mounted Punch	←+●
Angry Stomp	✕
Flip Splash	↓+✕
Double Knee Drop	←+✕
Flip Splash	↑+✕
Double Knee Drop	→+✕
Lower Body	
Raise Opponent	●
Toss	↑+●
Kick to Leg	→+●
Knee Stomp	←+●
Turnbuckle Moves	
Facing Opponent	
Irish Whip to Ropes	●
Shoulder Thrusts	←+●/→+●
Frankensteiner	↓+●/↑+●
Behind Opponent	
Irish Whip to Ropes	●
Super Back Drop	←+●/→+●
Super Back Drop	↓+●/↑+●
Opponent Sitting in Lower Turnbuckle	
Raise Opponent	●
Foot Choke	←+●/→+●
Foot Choke	↓+●/↑+●
Spinning Wheel Kick	▲+✕
Turnbuckle Attacks	
Opponent Standing	
Double Axe Handle	✕
Missile Dropkick	←+✕/→+✕
Missile Dropkick	↓+✕/↑+✕
Opponent on Mat	
Twisting Knee Drop	✕
Diving Moonsault	←+✕/→+✕
The 450	↓+✕/↑+✕
Running Attacks	
Facing Opponent	
Neckbreaker	●
Spear	←+●/→+●
Spear	↓+●/↑+●
Spinning Wheel Kick	✕
Back Elbow Attack	←+✕/→+✕
Back Elbow Attack	↓+✕/↑+✕
Behind Opponent	
School Boy	●
School Boy	←+●/→+●
School Boy	↓+●/↑+●
Running Counterattacks—Opponent Running	
Monkey Toss	●
Powerslam	←+●/→+●
Powerslam	↓+●/↑+●

DID YOU KNOW?

If Jeff's not strutting his stuff inside the squared circle, there's a good chance you'[l] him out on the dance floor showing off his moves.

School Boy

↓+● / ←+● / →+● / ↑+●

running at an opponen[t]
from behind

Scoop Slam

→+●

in front of opponent

Twisting Knee Drop

×

from the turnbuckle

Senton Bomb

L1

opponent on mat, from the turnbuckle

Hardy Boyz

Kane

Moves

ACTION	CONTROL
Facing the Opponent	
Irish Whip to Ropes	●
Stomach Crusher	↓+●
Hard Scoop Slam	←+●
Lifting Chokehold	↑+●
Side Buster	→+●
Body Punch	✕
Clothesline	↓+✕
Chop	←+✕
Kane Throat Thrust	↑+✕
Big Boot	→+✕
Facing the Groggy Opponent	
Tombstone Piledriver	↓+●
Pendulum Backbreaker	←+●
Spinebuster	↑+●
Manhattan Drop	→+●
Behind the Opponent	
Irish Whip to Ropes	●
Diving Reverse DDT	↓+●
Reverse Brainbuster	←+●
Full Nelson Slam	↑+●
Back Drop	→+●
Opponent on Mat	
Upper Body	
Raise Opponent	●
Sleeper Hold	↑+●
Camel Clutch	→+●
Darkness Choke	←+●
Angry Stomp	✕
Elbow Drop	↓+✕
Angry Stomp	←+✕
Elbow Drop	↑+✕
Angry Stomp	→+✕
Lower Body	
Raise Opponent	●
Knee Stomp	↑+●
Kick to Leg	→+●
Kick to Leg	←+●
Turnbuckle Moves	
Facing Opponent	
Irish Whip to Ropes	●
Choke	←+●/→+●
Mudhole Stomping	↓+●/↑+●
Behind Opponent	
Irish Whip to Ropes	●
Super Back Drop	←+●/→+●
Super Back Drop	↓+●/↑+●
Opponent Sitting in Lower Turnbuckle	
Raise Opponent	●
Foot Choke	←+●/→+●
Foot Choke	↓+●/↑+●
Shoulder Block	▲+✕
Turnbuckle Attacks	
Opponent Standing	
Double Axe Handle	✕
Flying Clothesline	←+✕/→+✕
Flying Clothesline	↓+✕/↑+✕
Opponent on Mat	
Elbow Drop	✕
Elbow Drop	←+✕/→+✕
Elbow Drop	↓+✕/↑+✕
Running Attacks	
Facing Opponent	
Neckbreaker Drop	●
Neckbreaker	←+●/→+●
Neckbreaker	↓+●/↑+●
Clothesline	✕
Shoulder Block	←+✕/→+✕
Shoulder Block	↓+✕/↑+✕
Behind Opponent	
Bulldog	●
Bulldog	←+●/→+●
Bulldog	↓+●/↑+●
Running Counterattacks—Opponent Running	
Monkey Toss	●
Powerslam	←+●/→+●
Powerslam	↓+●/↑+●

Height: 7'0"
Weight: 326 lbs.
Finishing Move: Tombstone Piledriver
Career Highlights: World Wrestling Federation Champion, Tag Team Champion

BIOGRAPHY

It's no wonder that when Kane entered the World Wrestling Federation, he did so in such an angry manner. If your brother tried to kill you when you were a kid, and the only person you interacted with for the past 20 years was Paul Bearer (who turned out to be your father), odds are you would be ready to tear through a steel cage, too.

Although Kane's arrival was no surprise—Paul Bearer had been promising it for weeks—the world was left speechless at first sight of him. Not only was he a monstrous, fearsome sight, but also behind his mask hid the pain of two decades of psychological torture.

Since Kane was unleashed on the world, his emotional growth has been immeasurable. If you're able to ignore his unbelievable size, you realize he is much like a young child going through the early stages of development. Learning as he goes, the Big Red Machine has been taught many hard lessons since allowing himself to be vulnerable to human emotions.

But don't be fooled. Kane may be learning the value of interpersonal relationships with friends and loved ones, but he's already mastered the art of interpersonal annihilation. The owner of an incredible physique, Kane also has the ability to incorporate high-flying maneuvers into his offense—an unexpected complement to his dominating power.

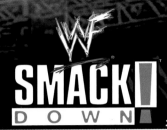

DID YOU KNOW?
Kane's hometown gym was going out of business recently, so he bought it and kept it open!

Stomach Crush
↓+●

in front of opponent

Big Boot
→+✕

in front of opponent

Lifting Chokeh
↑+●

in front of opponen

Choke Slam
L1

KANE

Ken Shamrock

Height: 6'1"
Weight: 235 lbs.
From: Sacramento, CA
Favorite Quote: "I'm in the Zone!"
Finishing Move: Ankle Lock Submission
Career Highlights: Intercontinental Champion, Tag Team Champion, 1998 King of the Ring®

BIOGRAPHY

ABC Television doesn't call you the "World's Most Dangerous Man" for nothing. You have to do a little something to earn that distinction. We think that becoming the Ultimate Fighting Champion (UFC) by defeating some of the toughest men in the world certainly qualifies as a "little something."

To become a champion in the UFC, it takes more than strength and mental awareness. You also need intensity, an unrelenting desire to be the best, and a lack of concern for your own personal safety. As you might have guessed, Shamrock possesses all of these qualities and more—which helped him make a smooth transition into becoming a World Wrestling Federation Superstar.

In a very short time, Shamrock developed his game from a bad-a$# into a bad-a$# who could also entertain us outside the ring, one who could compete in a match while tied up in a straightjacket, yet play the role of Mr. McMahon's personal enforcer. Kenny won over just as many fans with his consistent "snapping" (where he would tear about the area surrounding the ring and maybe even suplex a handful of WF officials if we were lucky!) as he did with his memorable victory at the 1998 King of the Ring® tournament.

One of the greatest things about Ken Shamrock is that there isn't only one fighting arena that he feels comfortable in...he feels right at home in all of them! An octagon, an Iron Circle, the catering room, the dressing room, and, oh yeah, even the ring.

Moves

ACTION	CONTROL
Facing the Opponent	
Irish Whip to Ropes	●
Belly to Back Flip	↓+●
Club to Neck	←+●
Dragon Screw	↑+●
Hurracanrana	→+●
Low Kick	✕
Clothesline	↓+✕
Middle Kick	←+✕
Body Punch	↑+✕
Back Elbow Smash	→+✕
Facing the Groggy Opponent	
Rolling Leg Lock	↓+●
Knee Strike	←+●
Flipping Armbar	↑+●
Fisherman Suplex	→+●
Behind the Opponent	
Irish Whip to Ropes	●
German Suplex Pin	↓+●
Back Drop	←+●
Sleeper Hold	↑+●
Back Side Slam	→+●
Opponent on Mat	
Upper Body	
Raise Opponent	●
Armbar	↑+●
Knee Smash	→+●
Mounted Punch	←+●
Angry Stomp	✕
Knee Drop	↓+✕
Angry Stomp	←+✕
Knee Drop	↑+✕
Angry Stomp	→+✕
Lower Body	
Raise Opponent	●
Knee Stomp	↑+●
Kick to Leg	→+●
Anklelock	←+●
Turnbuckle Moves	
Facing Opponent	
Irish Whip to Ropes	●
Shoulder Thrusts	←+●/→+●
Superplex	↓+●/↑+●
Behind Opponent	
Irish Whip to Ropes	●
Super Back Drop	←+●/→+●
Super Back Drop	↓+●/↑+●
Opponent Sitting in Lower Turnbuckle	
Raise Opponent	●
Foot Choke	←+●/→+●
Foot Choke	↓+●/↑+●
Back Elbow Attack	▲+✕
Turnbuckle Attacks	
Opponent Standing	
Double Axe Handle	✕
Double Axe Handle	←+✕/→+✕
Double Axe Handle	↓+✕/↑+✕
Opponent on Mat	
Elbow Drop	✕
Elbow Drop	←+✕/→+✕
Elbow Drop	↓+✕/↑+✕
Running Attacks	
Facing Opponent	
Spear	●
Spear	←+●/→+●
Spear	↓+●/↑+●
Back Elbow Attack	✕
Spinning Wheel Kick	←+✕/→+✕
Spinning Wheel Kick	↓+✕/↑+✕
Behind Opponent	
School Boy	●
School Boy	←+●/→+●
School Boy	↓+●/↑+●
Running Counterattacks—Opponent Running	
Monkey Toss	●
Powerslam	←+●/→+●
Powerslam	↓+●/↑+●

DID YOU KNOW?

Mick and The Rock aren't the only authors in the WWF. Kenny co-authored a book two years ago. Its name? Why, "Inside the Lion's Den" of course!

Mounted Pun

←+●

with opponent on ma

Dragon Screw

↑+●

in front of opponent

Hurracanra

→+●

in front of opponen

Shamrock Ankle Lock

L1

in front of opponent

THE WORLD'S
KEN SHAMROCK
MOST DANGEROUS MAN

Mankind

Height: 6'2"
Weight: 287 lbs.
Favorite Quote: "Have a nice day!"
Finishing Move: Mandible Claw
Career Highlights: World Wrestling Federation Champion, Tag Team Champion, Hardcore Champion

BIOGRAPHY

Take a walk over to your World Wrestling Federation® Home Video library and take out a tape from two years ago. Look at Mankind. Listen to what he says. Observe how he acts. Compare him to the Mankind you see now. Notice the differences.

Mick Foley has allowed his Mankind character to come full circle. Once a disturbed psychopath with a love for self-mutilation, Mankind has now become a lot of "fun." Dressed in his usual sweatpants, mask, shirt, and tie, Mankind is armed with an arsenal of hilarious one-liners every time he shows his face. His ever-present cotton sidekick, Mr. Socko, has quickly become one of the most popular inanimate objects to ever appear on television.

But don't get too comfortable with Mankind. Don't ever forget who he is. Although he makes it appear that his top talent these days may be as a comedic entertainer, Mankind will not hesitate to take a steel chair to his opponent's skull, get hardcore, and kick it old-school style. Windowpanes, 2x4s, thumbtacks, Mankind doesn't care...he'll use 'em all! The ring? That'll never be able to hold his extreme style!

To say Mankind is unique is perhaps the greatest understatement you could utter. How many people do you know who spend one day falling off a steel cage or taking multiple chair shots to the head, only to wake up the next morning (with a bad headache) to find out his autobiography has hit number one on the *New York Times* bestsellers list?

Moves

ACTION	CONTROL
Facing the Opponent	
Irish Whip to Ropes	●
Manhattan Drop	↓+●
DDT	←+●
Eye Rake	↑+●
Scoop Slam	→+●
Austin Punches	✕
Clothesline	↓+✕
Toe Kick	←+✕
Body Punch	↑+✕
Chop	→+✕
Facing the Groggy Opponent	
Jackknife Powerbomb	↓+●
Double Arm DDT	←+●
Pulling Piledriver	↑+●
Hard Scoop Slam	→+●
Behind the Opponent	
Irish Whip to Ropes	●
School Boy	↓+●
Facecrusher	←+●
Diving Reverse DDT	↑+●
Back Drop	→+●
Opponent on Mat	
Upper Body	
Raise Opponent	●
Mounted Punch	↑+●
Sleeper Hold	→+●
Camel Clutch	←+●
Angry Stomp	✕
Elbow Drop	↓+✕
Leg Drop	←+✕
Elbow Drop	↑+✕
Leg Drop	→+✕
Lower Body	
Raise Opponent	●
Leg Lock	↑+●
Toss	→+●
Knee Stomp	←+●
Turnbuckle Moves	
Facing Opponent	
Irish Whip to Ropes	●
10 Punch	←+●/→+●
Mudhole Stomping	↓+●/↑+●
Behind Opponent	
Irish Whip to Ropes	●
Super Back Drop	←+●/→+●
Super Back Drop	↓+●/↑+●
Opponent Sitting in Lower Turnbuckle	
Raise Opponent	●
Choke	←+●/→+●
Choke	↓+●/↑+●
Clothesline	▲+✕
Turnbuckle Attacks	
Opponent Standing	
Double Axe Handle	✕
Front Dropkick	←+✕/→+✕
Front Dropkick	↓+✕/↑+✕
Opponent on Mat	
Elbow Drop	✕
Knee Drop	←+✕/→+✕
Knee Drop	↓+✕/↑+✕
Running Attacks	
Facing Opponent	
Neckbreaker	●
Neckbreaker	←+●/→+●
Neckbreaker	↓+●/↑+●
Clothesline	✕
Shoulder Block	←+✕/→+✕
Shoulder Block	↓+✕/↑+✕
Behind Opponent	
Facecrusher	●
School Boy	←+●/→+●
School Boy	↓+●/↑+●
Running Counterattacks—Opponent Running	
Monkey Toss	●
Powerslam	←+●/→+●
Powerslam	↓+●/↑+●

DID YOU KNOW?

Mick Foley loves amusement parks and whenever there is one around the town where the WF is performing, he makes sure to stop by for a quick visit.

Powerslam

↓+● / ←+● / →+● / ↑+●

with opponent running at you

Find Socko

D-Pad+L2

behind opponent

Double Arm DDT

←+●

in front of a groggy opponent

[Mandible Claw

L1

MANKIND™

Mark Henry

Height: 6'1"
Weight: 380 lbs.
From: Silsby, TX
Finishing Move: Bearhug
Career Highlights: European Champion

BIOGRAPHY

Some people think that Mark Henry has a serious issue he needs help with, yet others feel his only problem is that there's only so much of him to go around!

A former Olympian, "Sexual Chocolate's" love for physical intimacy is as great as his need for competition. Claiming that he thinks about woman and sex "all the time," Henry's desires have caused him a number of problems in the past. A session of intense physical torture at the hands of Terri and a lifetime of emotional trauma thanks to Chyna have been consequences of Mark's overactive libido.

Whether it's the squared circle or the love arena, one thing is for certain—"Sexual Chocolate's" got game! A big man with a babyface and impeccable smile, Henry's poetic artistry has been known to win over a few of the ladies. Between the ropes, Mark relies on the power that earned him a successful showing as powerlifter in the 1996 Summer Olympics as a means to dominate his opponents.

Although Mark Henry nearly captured the Tag Team Title with D'Lo Brown on a number of occasions, and even enjoyed a run as the European Champion, many WWF insiders feel "Sexual Chocolate" has not even come close to tapping his enormous potential.

Moves

ACTION	CONTROL
Facing the Opponent	
Irish Whip to Ropes	●
Arm Wrench	↓+●
Hard Scoop Slam	←+●
Club to Neck	↑+●
Side Buster	→+●
Chop	✕
Clothesline	↓+✕
Toe Kick	←+✕
Double Axe Handle	↑+✕
Overhand Punch	→+✕
Facing the Groggy Opponent	
Body Press Drop Forward	↓+●
Pendulum Back Breaker	←+●
Body Press Slam	↑+●
Side Buster	→+●
Behind the Opponent	
Irish Whip to Ropes	●
Back Side Slam	↓+●
Back Drop	←+●
Full Nelson Slam	↑+●
Atomic Drop	→+●
Opponent on Mat	
Upper Body	
Raise Opponent	●
Sleeper Hold	↑+●
Knee Smash	→+●
Camel Clutch	←+●
Angry Stomp	✕
Angry Stomp	↓+✕
Angry Stomp	←+✕
Angry Stomp	↑+✕
Angry Stomp	→+✕
Lower Body	
Raise Opponent	●
Boston Crab	↑+●
Toss	→+●
Leg Lock	←+●
Turnbuckle Moves	
Facing Opponent	
Irish Whip to Ropes	●
Choke	←+●/→+●
Shoulder Thrusts	↓+●/↑+●
Behind Opponent	
Irish Whip to Ropes	●
Super Back Drop	←+●/→+●
Super Back Drop	↓+●/↑+●
Opponent Sitting in Lower Turnbuckle	
Raise Opponent	●
Choke	←+●/→+●
Choke	↓+●/↑+●
Shoulder Block	▲+✕
Turnbuckle Attacks	
Opponent Standing	
Double Axe Handle	✕
Double Axe Handle	←+✕/→+✕
Double Axe Handle	↓+✕/↑+✕
Opponent on Mat	
Elbow Drop	✕
Elbow Drop	←+✕/→+✕
Elbow Drop	↓+✕/↑+✕
Running Attacks	
Facing Opponent	
Neckbreaker	●
Neckbreaker	←+●/→+●
Neckbreaker	↓+●/↑+●
Shoulder Block	✕
Clothesline	←+✕/→+✕
Clothesline	↓+✕/↑+✕
Behind Opponent	
Bulldog	●
Bulldog	←+●/→+●
Bulldog	↓+●/↑+●
Running Counterattacks—Opponent Running	
Monkey Toss	●
Powerslam	←+●/→+●
Powerslam	↓+●/↑+●

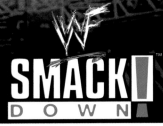
DID YOU KNOW?

Competing against some of the greatest athletes in the world, Mark Henry dunked on a regulation rim during the *Foot Locker Slam Dunk Championship,* and earned a perfect score and standing ovation from the crowd.

Body Press Slam

↑+●

in front of groggy opponent

Diving Body Press

×

from the turnbuckle opponent out of ring

Atomic Drop

→+●

from behind opponent

Bearhug

L1

MARK HENRY™

NET WT. 400 lbs. **SEXUAL CHOCOLATE**

Moves

ACTION	CONTROL
Facing the Opponent	
Irish Whip to Ropes	●
Arm Wrench	↓+●
Scoop Slam	←+●
Suplex	↑+●
Scissors Sweep	→+●
Snap Jab	✕
Dropkick	↓+✕
Back Elbow Smash	←+✕
Rolling Wheel Kick	↑+✕
Chop	→+✕
Facing the Groggy Opponent	
Rib Breaker	↓+●
Falling Neckbreaker	←+●
Stomach Crusher	↑+●
DDT	→+●
Behind the Opponent	
Irish Whip to Ropes	●
Diving Reverse DDT	↓+●
Back Drop	←+●
Sleeper Hold	↑+●
German Suplex Pin	→+●
Opponent on Mat	
Upper Body	
Raise Opponent	●
Knee Smash	↑+●
Reverse Chin Lock	→+●
Mounted Punch	←+●
Angry Stomp	✕
Leg Drop	↓+✕
Elbow Drop	←+✕
Austin Elbow Drop	↑+✕
Angry Stomp	→+✕
Lower Body	
Raise Opponent	●
Pin with Bridge	↑+●
Leg Lock	→+●
Knee Stomp	←+●
Turnbuckle Moves	
Facing Opponent	
Irish Whip to Ropes	●
Mudhole Stomping	←+●/→+●
Tornado DDT	↓+●/↑+●
Behind Opponent	
Irish Whip to Ropes	●
Super Back Drop	←+●/→+●
Super Back Drop	↓+●/↑+●
Opponent Sitting in Lower Turnbuckle	
Raise Opponent	●
Foot Choke	←+●/→+●
Foot Choke	↓+●/↑+●
Diving Forearm Smash	▲+✕
Turnbuckle Attacks	
Opponent Standing	
Double Axe Handle	✕
Spinning Wheel Kick	←+✕/→+✕
Spinning Wheel Kick	↓+✕/↑+✕
Opponent on Mat	
Senton Bomb	✕
Knee Drop	←+✕/→+✕
Diving Moonsault	↓+✕/↑+✕
Running Attacks	
Facing Opponent	
Neckbreaker Drop	●
Neckbreaker	←+●/→+●
Neckbreaker	↓+●/↑+●
Diving Forearm Smash	✕
Power Clothesline	←+✕/→+✕
Power Clothesline	↓+✕/↑+✕
Behind Opponent	
Bulldog	●
Bulldog	←+●/→+●
Bulldog	↓+●/↑+●
Running Counterattacks—Opponent Running	
Monkey Toss	
Samoan Drop	←+●/→+●
Samoan Drop	↓+●/↑+●

Matt Hardy

Matt Hardy

Height: 6'1"
Weight: 227 lbs.
From: Cameron, NC
Finishing Move: Splash/Leg Drop combo
Career Highlights: Tag Team Champion

BIOGRAPHY

Can you really refer to a Superstar who's not even in his mid-20's as the "veteran leader" of his team? Ninty-seven percent of the time, the answer to this question is a resounding "no," but when you're talking about Matt Hardy we all know what the answer is.

Growing up in North Carolina and awed by the allure of the "big time," Matt was driven to land in the World Wrestling Federation. Alongside his talented younger brother, Jeff Hardy, Matt was able to achieve his initial goal, but he couldn't have imagined how far he would take it.

After only a few short months, they were veterans in the WWF, and Matt guided the brothers to a lifelong dream—capturing the Tag Team Titles in their home state! When they were younger, the Hardy brothers spent day after day role playing this scenario, and in July of 1999 it came to fruition.

As the elder statesman for the most athletic tag team to come along in years, Matt Hardy has been forced to grow up at a much quicker pace than your average WWF rookie. When they're in the ring, Matt and Jeff share the responsibility of amazing the crowd, but behind the curtain, Matt takes control. And what a great job he has done.

The result of an honorable upbringing and tireless practice, Matt Hardy is on the fast track to the top!

DID YOU KNOW?

When he and his brother were working as independent wrestlers, Matt supplemented their income by designing other guys' wrestling attire.

Diving Reverse DDT

↓+●

behind the opponent

Suplex

↑+●

in front of opponent

Rolling Wheel Kick

↑+✕

in front of opponent

Northern Lights Suplex

L1

Mr. ASS

Height: 6'4"
Weight: 270 lbs.
From: Austin, TX
Favorite Quote: "If you're not down with that, I got two words for ya!"
Finishing Move: Fame-Asser
Career Highlights: Tag Team Champion, Hardcore Champion, 1999 King of the Ring®

BIOGRAPHY

It's been said time and again that Badd Ass Billy Gunn may be the best all-around athlete the World Wrestling Federation has ever seen. His imposing physique adds an enormous amount of power to an offensive repertoire, which—thanks to his athleticism—is as diverse as they come.

A problem that Mr. Ass has run into has to do with his natural athletic ability. It's not always his most dominating feature. Equipped with an ego large enough to fill most of the contiguous 48 states, Mr. Ass never has a difficult time finding enemies. The problem isn't that he's good, the problem is that he knows how good he is and loves to talk about it!

As a member of the New Age Outlaws, Mr. Ass was part of the most successful tag team the Federation has ever seen. Not only have he and the Road Dogg won the WF Tag Team Titles on numerous occasions, but they also share a special chemistry that has made them one of the most entertaining and beloved duos in history. And let's not forget Mr. Ass' contribution to D-Generation X, the most influential and controversial group in history.

When the time came for Mr. Ass to separate from his partner and fellow D-Generates, singles success was not hard to come by. The 1999 King of the Ring® also enjoyed a run as the Hardcore Champion and several near misses at the Intercontinental Title.

In the ring and out of it, Badd Ass Billy Gunn is one Superstar who has done it all and succeeded!

Moves

ACTION	CONTROL
Facing the Opponent	
Irish Whip to Ropes	●
Arm Wrench	↓+●
Headlock and Punch	←+●
Brainbuster	↑+●
Club to Neck	→+●
Snap Jab	×
Dropkick	↓+×
Toe Kick	←+×
Double Axe Handle	↑+×
Chop	→+×
Facing the Groggy Opponent	
Piledriver	↓+●
Falling Neckbreaker	←+●
Body Press Slam	↑+●
DDT	→+●
Behind the Opponent	
Irish Whip to Ropes	●
Atomic Drop	↓+●
Bulldog	←+●
Back Drop	↑+●
Russian Leg Sweep	→+●
Opponent on Mat	
Upper Body	
Raise Opponent	●
Camel Clutch	↑+●
Reverse Chin Lock	→+●
Mounted Punch	←+●
Angry Stomp	×
Austin Elbow Drop	↓+×
Knee Drop	←+×
Austin Elbow Drop	↑+×
Knee Drop	→+×
Lower Body	
Raise Opponent	●
Kick to Leg	↑+●
Toss	→+●
Leg Lock	←+●
Turnbuckle Moves	
Facing Opponent	
Irish Whip to Ropes	●
Shoulder Thrusts	←+●/→+●
Tornado DDT	↓+●/↑+●
Behind Opponent	
Irish Whip to Ropes	●
Super Back Drop	←+●/→+●
Super Back Drop	↓+●/↑+●
Opponent Sitting in Lower Turnbuckle	
Raise Opponent	●
Foot Choke	←+●/→+●
Foot Choke	↓+●/↑+●
Back Elbow Attack	▲+×
Turnbuckle Attacks	
Opponent Standing	
Double Axe Handle	×
Diving Fame Asser	←+×/→+×
Diving Fame Asser	↓+×/↑+×
Opponent on Mat	
Knee Drop	×
Elbow Drop	←+×/→+×
Elbow Drop	↓+×/↑+×
Running Attacks	
Facing Opponent	
Rolling Clutch Pin	●
Neckbreaker	←+●/→+●
Neckbreaker	↓+●/↑+●
Back Elbow Attack	×
Dropkick	←+×/→+×
Dropkick	↓+×/↑+×
Behind Opponent	
Bulldog	●
School Boy	←+●/→+●
School Boy	↓+●/↑+●
Running Counterattacks—Opponent Running	
Monkey Toss	●
Powerslam	←+●/→+●
Powerslam	↓+●/↑+●

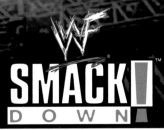

Prima's Official Strategy G

DID YOU KNOW?

Most of his peers consider Badd Ass Billy Gunn the most talented basketball player in the locker room.

Tornado DD

↓+● / ↑+●

opponent in the turnbu**

Brainbuster

↑+●

in front of opponent

Atomic Dro

↓+●

behind the oppone**

Fame Asser

L1

MR ASS

Paul Bearer

Favorite Quote:
"I'm Paul Bearer and you're not!"

BIOGRAPHY

Throughout his illustrious career with the Undertaker, Paul Bearer served as the perfect complement to the Phenom.

Tall, muscular, silent and mysterious, the Lord of Darkness has dominated much of the Federation roster for the past few years. And usually in his corner was the short, overweight, boisterous Paul Bearer. Equipped with a voice that could shatter a windshield, Bearer never seemed to keep quiet. That wouldn't have been so bad, but it also meant that we had to look at his rather large and often disturbing face. But weird as they may be, there's no doubt that some of Bearer's facial expressions rank right up there with the best of them!

As the co-mastermind behind many of the Undertaker's vicious schemes, Bearer was in the forefront of the WF for some time. But when the Undertaker was forced to step away for a short time, Bearer went with him.

But now the duo is back...and what a changed man Paul Bearer is. Of course his intentions are still pure evil, but he shed a considerable amount of weight, so the nickname "Fat Man" cannot be thrown his way again!

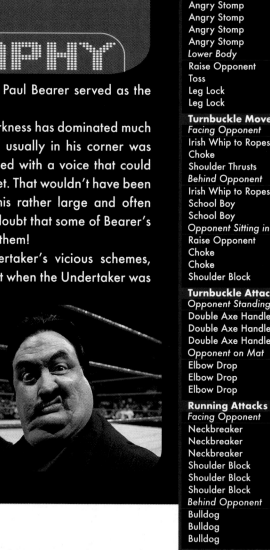

ACTION	Moves	CONTROL
Facing the Opponent		
Irish Whip to Ropes		●
Club to Neck		↓+●
Snapmare		←+●
Eye Rake		↑+●
Club to Neck		→+●
Chop		✕
Body Punch		↓+✕
Toe Kick		←+✕
Double Axe Handle		↑+✕
Austin Punches		→+✕
Facing the Groggy Opponent		
Piledriver		↓+●
Snapmare		←+●
Scoop Slam		↑+●
Club to Neck		→+●
Behind the Opponent		
Irish Whip to Ropes		●
Reverse Pin		↓+●
Turn Facing Front		←+●
Reverse Pin		↑+●
Turn to Face		→+●
Opponent on Mat		
Upper Body		
Raise Opponent		●
Sleeper Hold		↑+●
Knee Smash		→+●
Knee Smash		←+●
Angry Stomp		✕
Angry Stomp		↓+✕
Angry Stomp		←+✕
Angry Stomp		↑+✕
Angry Stomp		→+✕
Lower Body		
Raise Opponent		●
Toss		↑+●
Leg Lock		→+●
Leg Lock		←+●
Turnbuckle Moves		
Facing Opponent		
Irish Whip to Ropes		●
Choke		←+●/→+●
Shoulder Thrusts		↓+●/↑+●
Behind Opponent		
Irish Whip to Ropes		●
School Boy		←+●/→+●
School Boy		↓+●/↑+●
Opponent Sitting in Lower Turnbuckle		
Raise Opponent		●
Choke		←+●/→+●
Choke		↓+●/↑+●
Shoulder Block		▲+✕
Turnbuckle Attacks		
Opponent Standing		
Double Axe Handle		✕
Double Axe Handle		←+✕/→+✕
Double Axe Handle		↓+✕/↑+✕
Opponent on Mat		
Elbow Drop		✕
Elbow Drop		←+✕/→+✕
Elbow Drop		↓+✕/↑+✕
Running Attacks		
Facing Opponent		
Neckbreaker		●
Neckbreaker		←+●/→+●
Neckbreaker		↓+●/↑+●
Shoulder Block		✕
Shoulder Block		←+✕/→+✕
Shoulder Block		↓+✕/↑+✕
Behind Opponent		
Bulldog		●
Bulldog		←+●/→+●
Bulldog		↓+●/↑+●

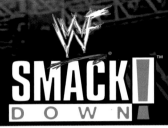

DID YOU KNOW?

As a kid growing up, he and his best friend used to pretend to be professiona wrestlers. His friend's name—Michael Hayes!

Diving Body Press

×

from the turnbuckle
opponent out of ring

Reverse Pin

↓+●/↑+●

from behind opponent

Toss

↑+●

opponent on groun
lower body

DDT

L1

Paul Bearer

Road Dogg

Height: 6'2"
Weight: 236 lbs.
From: Nashville, TN
Favorite Quote:
"Oh, you didn't know?!"
Finishing Move: Pumphandle Slam
Career Highlights: Tag Team Champion,
Hardcore Champion, Intercontinental
Champion

BIOGRAPHY

There's a very slight chance that in 50 years you might somehow forget the Road Dogg's face. But there is absolutely no chance that you will ever forget his voice!

If you've ever been to a World Wrestling Federation live event or watched one of the programs (we're assuming you have), then we're certain you'll agree that the Road Dogg's trademark entrance is one of the most entertaining parts of the show. With his unforgettable voice and enough charisma to win the Presidency of the United States, the D-O-Double-G always gets the crowd up on their feet and singing along with him.

Of course, these fun and games would all be meaningless if the Road Dogg couldn't back up his showmanship with a bit of brawlin'. An accomplished Hardcore competitor, Road Dogg is all business once he steps in between the ropes. With numerous Tag Team Title reigns, an Intercontinental Title reign, a Hardcore Title reign, and starring roles in some of the Federation's most memorable vignettes, the Road Dogg has solidified his place as one of the most accomplished all-around Superstars to ever compete in the World Wrestling Federation!

ACTION	Moves	CONTROL
Facing the Opponent		
Irish Whip to Ropes		●
Jumping Arm Breaker		↓+●
Snapmare		←+●
Stomach Crusher		↑+●
Double Arm Suplex		→+●
Shake Jab		✕
Body Punch		↓+✕
Snap Jab		←+✕
Clothesline		↑+✕
Chop		→+✕
Facing the Groggy Opponent		
Piledriver		↓+●
DDT		←+●
Jackknife Powerbomb		↑+●
Fall Away Slam		→+●
Behind the Opponent		
Irish Whip to Ropes		●
School Boy		↓+●
Back Drop		←+●
Sleeper Hold		↑+●
Facecrusher		→+●
Opponent on Mat		
Upper Body		
Raise Opponent		●
Knee Smash		↑+●
Sleeper Hold		→+●
Mounted Punch		←+●
Angry Stomp		✕
Angry Stomp		↓+✕
Shaky Knee Drop		←+✕
Angry Stomp		↑+✕
Shaky Knee Drop		→+✕
Lower Body		
Raise Opponent		●
Leg Lock		↑+●
Kick to Leg		→+●
Knee Stomp		←+●
Turnbuckle Moves		
Facing Opponent		
Irish Whip to Ropes		●
10 Punch		←+●/→+●
Mudhole Stomping		↓+●/↑+●
Behind Opponent		
Irish Whip to Ropes		●
Super Back Drop		←+●/→+●
Super Back Drop		↓+●/↑+●
Opponent Sitting in Lower Turnbuckle		
Raise Opponent		●
Foot Choke		←+●/→+●
Foot Choke		↓+●/↑+●
Clothesline		▲+✕
Turnbuckle Attacks		
Opponent Standing		
Double Axe Handle		✕
Missile Dropkick		←+✕/→+✕
Missile Dropkick		↓+✕/↑+✕
Opponent on Mat		
Knee Drop		✕
Knee Drop		←+✕/→+✕
Knee Drop		↓+✕/↑+✕
Running Attacks		
Facing Opponent		
Rolling Clutch Pin		●
Neckbreaker Drop		←+●/→+●
Neckbreaker Drop		↓+●/↑+●
Clothesline		✕
Back Elbow Attack		←+✕/→+✕
Back Elbow Attack		↓+✕/↑+✕
Behind Opponent		
Facecrusher		●
School Boy		←+●/→+●
School Boy		↓+●/↑+●

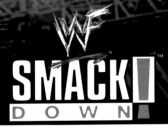

DID YOU KNOW?

Thanks to his infamous entrance, the Road Dogg has been approached to recor studio album where he would be the featured voice.

Double Arm Suplex

→+●

in front of opponent

Stomach Crusher

↑+●

in front of opponent

Shake, Rattle & Roll

×,×,×,×

in front of opponent

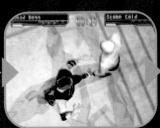

Pumphandle Slam

L1

behind opponent

The Rock

Height: 6'5"
Weight: 275 lbs.
From: Miami, FL
Favorite Quote: "It Doesn't Matter..."
Finishing Move: People's Elbow
Career Highlights: World Wrestling Federation Champion, Intercontinental Champion, Tag Team Champion

BIOGRAPHY

He is simply electrifying.

Combining immeasurable amounts of athleticism and charisma, The People's Champ has the ability to stir thousands of fans into a crazed frenzy with just one word or the raise of an eyebrow.

"The Great One" is the personification of "cool." Good looking, well dressed, and intelligent, The Rock always seems to come out on top. It's no wonder that everyone walks around wanting to be like The Rock. And now with WF SmackDown!™ at your side, you can turn on your PlayStation...hit the proper buttons...choose The Rock as the Superstar you'll play with...listen for his music, ("If Ya' Smelllalala")...but before you lock up with your competition...take a good look at that controller you're about to play with...memorize where the buttons are...get a good feel for it...take out your little handkerchief...shine it up real nice...turn that sunbitch sideways and stick it straight up your opponent's candy a$#!

Does that line sound familiar to you? It doesn't matter if that line sounds familiar to you! Just plug in WF SmackDown!™, choose The Rock and watch the millions and millions of The Rock's fans cheer you on to the World Wrestling Federation Championship!

If ya' smell what The Rock is cookin'!

Moves

ACTION	CONTROL
Facing the Opponent	
Irish Whip to Ropes	●
DDT	↓+●
Scoop Slam	←+●
Eye Rake	↑+●
Club to Neck	→+●
Rock Punches	✕
Clothesline	↓+✕
Toe Kick	←+✕
Double Axe Handle	↑+✕
Elbow Smash	→+✕
Facing the Groggy Opponent	
Manhattan Drop	↓+●
The Rock Bottom	←+●
Suplex	↑+●
Jumping Swinging DDT	→+●
Behind the Opponent	
Irish Whip to Ropes	●
Atomic Drop	↓+●
Back Drop	←+●
Sleeper Hold	↑+●
Russian Leg Sweep	→+●
Opponent on Mat	
Upper Body	
Raise Opponent	●
Mounted Punch	↑+●
Sleeper Hold	→+●
Knee Smash	←+●
Angry Stomp	✕
Angry Stomp	↓+✕
Rock Stomp	←+✕
Angry Stomp	↑+✕
Rock Stomp	→+✕
Lower Body	
Raise Opponent	●
Toss	↑+●
Leg Lock	→+●
Kick to Leg	←+●
Turnbuckle Moves	
Facing Opponent	
Irish Whip to Ropes	●
Shoulder Thrusts	←+●/→+●
Superplex	↓+●/↑+●
Behind Opponent	
Irish Whip to Ropes	●
Super Back Drop	←+●/→+●
Super Back Drop	↓+●/↑+●
Opponent Sitting in Lower Turnbuckle	
Raise Opponent	●
Foot Choke	←+●/→+●
Foot Choke	↓+●/↑+●
Clothesline	▲+✕
Turnbuckle Attacks	
Opponent Standing	
Double Axe Handle	✕
Double Axe Handle	←+✕/→+✕
Double Axe Handle	↓+✕/↑+✕
Opponent on Mat	
Elbow Drop	✕
Knee Drop	←+✕/→+✕
Knee Drop	↓+✕/↑+✕
Running Attacks	
Facing Opponent	
Neckbreaker	●
Neckbreaker	←+●/→+●
Neckbreaker	↓+●/↑+●
Clothesline	✕
Shoulder Block	←+✕/→+✕
Shoulder Block	↓+✕/↑+✕
Behind Opponent	
School Boy	●
School Boy	←+●/→+●
School Boy	↓+●/↑+●
Running Counter Attacks—Opponent Running	
Monkey Toss	●
Samoan Drop	←+●/→+●
Samoan Drop	↓+●/↑+●

DID YOU KNOW?

The Rock buys all of his "$500 shirts" at Lucky's, a store in his hometown of Mic

Russian Leg Sweep

→+●

behind an opponent

Toss

↑+●

opponent on mat, lower body

The Rock Bott

←+●

in front of groggy oppon

The People's Elbow

L1

opponent on mat
upper body

Moves

ACTION	CONTROL
Facing the Opponent	
Irish Whip to Ropes	●
Suplex	↓+●
Eye Rake	←+●
Scoop Slam	↑+●
Club to Neck	→+●
Snap Jab	✕
Body Punch	↓+✕
Toe Kick	←+✕
Double Axe Handle	↑+✕
Chop	→+✕
Facing the Groggy Opponent	
DDT	↓+●
Snapmare	←+●
Hard Scoop Slam	↑+●
Arm Wrench	→+●
Behind the Opponent	
Irish Whip to Ropes	●
School Boy	↓+●
Turn to Face	←+●
School Boy	↑+●
Turn to Face	→+●
Opponent on Mat	
Upper Body	
Raise Opponent	●
Sleeper Hold	↑+●
Knee Smash	→+●
Knee Smash	←+●
Angry Stomp	✕
Angry Stomp	↓+✕
Angry Stomp	←+✕
Angry Stomp	↑+✕
Angry Stomp	→+✕
Lower Body	
Raise Opponent	●
Knee Stomp	↑+●
Leg Lock	→+●
Leg Lock	←+●
Turnbuckle Moves	
Facing Opponent	
Irish Whip to Ropes	●
Mudhole Stomping	←+●/→+●
Shoulder Thrusts	↓+●/↑+●
Behind Opponent	
Irish Whip to Ropes	●
Super Back Drop	←+●/→+●
Super Back Drop	↓+●/↑+●
Opponent Sitting in Lower Turnbuckle	
Raise Opponent	●
Choke	←+●/→+●
Choke	↓+●/↑+●
Bronco Buster	▲+✕
Turnbuckle Attacks	
Opponent Standing	
Double Axe Handle	✕
Double Axe Handle	←+✕/→+✕
Double Axe Handle	↓+✕/↑+✕
Opponent on Mat	
Test Diving Elbow	✕
Dragon Attack	←+✕/→+✕
Dragon Attack	↓+✕/↑+✕
Running Attacks	
Facing Opponent	
Neckbreaker	●
Neckbreaker	←+●/→+●
Neckbreaker	↓+●/↑+●
Back Elbow Attack	✕
Bronco Buster	←+✕/→+✕
Bronco Buster	↓+✕/↑+✕
Behind Opponent	
Bulldog	●
Bulldog	←+●/→+●
Bulldog	↓+●/↑+●
Running Counterattacks—Opponent Running	
Monkey Toss	●
Powerslam	←+●/→+●
Powerslam	↓+●/↑+●

Height: 6'2"
Weight: 230 lbs.
From: Greenwich, CT
Finishing Move: Bronco Buster
Career Highlights: European Champion

BIOGRAPHY

Can you really blame Shane-O Mac for being a little arrogant? Growing up in Greenwich, Connecticut, as the son of Vince McMahon certainly lends itself to the belief that you are better than most everyone else. Could you imagine being a good-looking teenage boy, driving around in a $100,000 sports car while all the girls chased you? Neither can we. OK, enough about that. We're starting to get jealous.

Within months of appearing on WWF programming, there was no doubt that Shane had the confidence, intelligence, and cold-heartedness of his father, but the question remained, could he put it all together?

The answer to that question was a very big yes. With one leap off the top rope onto the Spanish announcer's table, Shane McMahon proved that he had inherited more than that "wind-tunnel tested hairdo" from his father. Taking his cue from Vince's amazing performances at the *Royal Rumble*® and *St. Valentine's Day Massacre*, Shane earned the respect he yearned for that day when he left his concerns in the ring and came crashing down on Test outside of it.

With the ability to compete in the most thrilling of matches, a killer wardrobe, and a million-dollar-smile with the charisma to match, we have the feeling Shane McMahon is going to be around for a long time. Actually, seeing as how he's the owner, we have the feeling that he's going to be around for a very long time, even if he didn't have all that going for him. But he does, so we don't have to have that feeling.

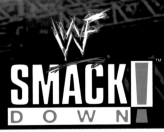

DID YOU KNOW?

Growing up, Shane was so protective of his sister that he would have his pals—
Mean Street Posse—keep tabs on her so he knew who she was hanging out wi[th]

Super Back Dr[op]

↓+● / ←+● / →+● / ↑+●

opponent in turnbuck[le]

Schoolboy

↓+● / ↑+●

from behind opponent

Bronco Bust[er]

↓+✕ / ←+✕ / →+✕ / ↑+✕

running attack
opponent in turnbuc[kle]

Test Diving Elbow

L1

from turnbuckle

opponent on mat

Shane McMahon™

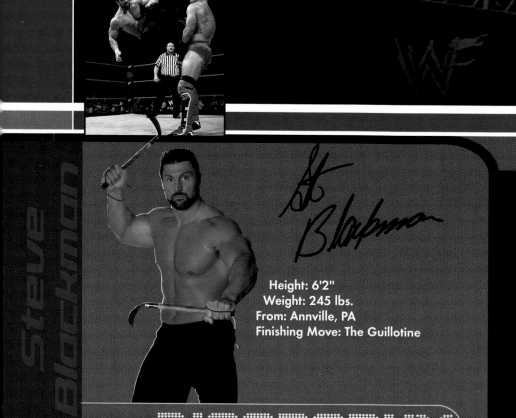

Steve Blackman

Height: 6'2"
Weight: 245 lbs.
From: Annville, PA
Finishing Move: The Guillotine

BIOGRAPHY

If silence were a weapon, Steve Blackman would be lethal. Hey, wait a minute...he *is* the Lethal Weapon!

Some Superstars rely on heavy verbal assault as a way of getting their opponents' attention. Blackman, on the other hand, takes the opposite route. Never one to utter many words, the Pennsylvania native realizes his strong points and takes advantage of them by attacking without making a sound.

In the amount of time most people take to get out a sentence, Blackman has the ability to drop his opponent to the canvas and force them into submission. He attacks with the efficiency of the martial arts expert he is, and Blackman's amazing control of his body allows him to use his extremities as feared weapons.

But if that doesn't work, he's always ready to take out his kendo stick and beat you silly with it.

Moves

ACTION	CONTROL
Facing the Opponent	
Irish Whip to Ropes	●
DDT	↓+●
Knee Strike	←+●
Eye Rake	↑+●
Scissor Sweep	→+●
Low Kick	✕
Dropkick	↓+✕
Toe Kick	←+✕
Shuffle Side Kick	↑+✕
Chop	→+✕
Facing the Groggy Opponent	
Piledriver	↓+●
Knee Strike	←+●
Shoulder Breaker	↑+●
Dragon Screw	→+●
Behind the Opponent	
Irish Whip to Ropes	●
Diving Reverse DDT	↓+●
Back Drop	←+●
Atomic Drop	↑+●
German Suplex Pin	→+●
Opponent on Mat	
Upper Body	
Raise Opponent	●
Knee Smash	↑+●
Sleeper Hold	→+●
Armbar	←+●
Angry Stomp	✕
Angry Stomp	↓+✕
Angry Stomp	←+✕
Angry Stomp	↑+✕
Angry Stomp	→+✕
Lower Body	
Raise Opponent	●
Kick to Leg	↑+●
Knee Stomp	→+●
Knee Stomp	←+●
Turnbuckle Moves	
Facing Opponent	
Irish Whip to Ropes	●
Foot Choke	←+●/→+●
Mudhole Stomping	↓+●/↑+●
Behind Opponent	
Irish Whip to Ropes	●
Super Back Drop	←+●/→+●
Super Back Drop	↓+●/↑+●
Opponent Sitting in Lower Turnbuckle	
Raise Opponent	●
Choke	←+●/→+●
Choke	↓+●/↑+●
Karate Kick	▲+✕
Turnbuckle Attacks	
Opponent Standing	
Double Axe Handle	✕
Front Dropkick	←+✕/→+✕
Front Dropkick	↓+✕/↑+✕
Opponent on Mat	
Elbow Drop	✕
Knee Drop	←+✕/→+✕
Knee Drop	↓+✕/↑+✕
Running Attacks	
Facing Opponent	
Spear	●
Spear	←+●/→+●
Spear	↓+●/↑+●
Karate Kick	✕
Diving Shoulder	←+✕/→+✕
Diving Shoulder	↓+✕/↑+✕
Behind Opponent	
School Boy	●
School Boy	←+●/→+●
School Boy	↓+●/↑+●
Running Counterattacks—Opponent Running	
Monkey Toss	●
Powerslam	←+●/→+●
Powerslam	↓+●/↑+●

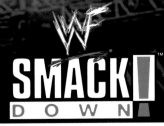

DID YOU KNOW?

Steve Blackman runs a martial arts training facility in his hometown.

Knee Strike

←+●

in front of opponent

Armbar

→+●

opponent on ground
upper body

Karate Kic

▲+✕

running attack

Fisherman Suplex

L1

Lethal Weapon
STEVE BLACKMAN

Stone Cold

Height: 6'2"
Weight: 252 lbs.
From: Victoria, TX
Favorite Quote: "And that's all I got to say about that!"
Finishing Move:
Stone Cold Stunner
Career Highlights: Federation Champion, Intercontinental Champion, Tag Team Champion, 1996 King of the Ring®, 1998 Royal Rumble® Winner

BIOGRAPHY

If you take a step back and look at Stone Cold Steve Austin, you'll realize why he is one of the most popular Superstars to ever compete in the World Wrestling Federation. When the Rattlesnake isn't busy stomping a mudhole in one of his peers, he's usually drinking beer, flipping someone off, or getting in his boss' face—and if you're real lucky, he'll be doing all three at the same time!

Anyone who has ever worked a day in their lives has fantasized about beating the arrogance out of their boss with a steel chair, calling him a jackass, or dumping a beer over his wind-tunnel-tested hairdo.

What makes Stone Cold Steve Austin the man that he is, is that he doesn't fantasize about doing these things (hell, the word fantasize probably never even passed his lips)—he just does them. Many times, older married men look at their younger, single counterparts and say, "Go out and have fun. I live vicariously through you."

This is how the typical Federation fan views Stone Cold. They think, "First, I'm going to destroy my adversary of the day (work). Then I'm going to grab the evil leader behind all of my problems (my boss) and annihilate him with uncontrolled fury. When it's all over and I'm standing on top a victorious man, I will celebrate with multiple beers as the world cheers me on."

What we wouldn't give to live one day in the life of Stone Cold Steve Austin.

Moves

ACTION	CONTROL
Facing the Opponent	
Irish Whip to Ropes	●
Side Buster	↓+●
Scoop Slam	←+●
Eye Rake	↑+●
Suplex	→+●
Austin Punches	✕
Clothesline	↓+✕
Snap Jab	←+✕
Overhand Punch	↑+✕
Toe Kick	→+✕
Facing the Groggy Opponent	
Side Buster	↓+●
Stunner	←+●
Piledriver	↑+●
DDT	→+●
Behind the Opponent	
Irish Whip to Ropes	●
Bulldog	↓+●
Back Drop	←+●
Sleeper Hold	↑+●
Turn to Face	→+●
Opponent on Mat	
Upper Body	
Raise Opponent	●
Sleeper Hold	↑+●
Mounted Punch	→+●
Mounted Punch	←+●
Angry Stomp	✕
Angry Stomp	↓+✕
Austin Elbow Drop	←+✕
Angry Stomp	↑+✕
Austin Elbow Drop	→+✕
Lower Body	
Raise Opponent	●
Toss	↑+●
Leg Lock	→+●
Kick to Groin	←+●
Turnbuckle Moves	
Facing Opponent	
Irish Whip to Ropes	●
Shoulder Thrusts	←+●/→+●
Foot Choke	↓+●/↑+●
Behind Opponent	
Irish Whip to Ropes	●
Super Back Drop	←+●/→+●
Super Back Drop	↓+●/↑+●
Opponent Sitting in Lower Turnbuckle	
Raise Opponent	●
Foot Choke	←+●/→+●
Foot Choke	↓+●/↑+●
Power Clothesline	▲+✕
Turnbuckle Attacks	
Opponent Standing	
Double Axe Handle	✕
Double Axe Handle	←+✕/→+✕
Double Axe Handle	↓+✕/↑+✕
Opponent on Mat	
Diving Elbow	✕
Diving Elbow	←+✕/→+✕
Diving Elbow	↓+✕/↑+✕
Running Attacks	
Facing Opponent	
Press and Knuckle	●
Press and Knuckle	←+●/→+●
Press and Knuckle	↓+●/↑+●
Power Clothesline	✕
Shoulder Block	←+✕/→+✕
Shoulder Block	↓+✕/↑+✕
Behind Opponent	
Bulldog	●
Bulldog	←+●/→+●
Bulldog	↓+●/↑+●

DID YOU KNOW?

Minnesota Viking superstar John Randle received national media attention because he preferred to wear the infamous "Austin 3:16" T-shirt during pre-game stretches to help him get psyched up.

Side Buster

↓ + ●

facing an opponent

Austin Punches

×

a standing opponent

Austin Elbow Drop

×

with opponent on mat

Stone Cold Stunner

L1

Test

Height: 6'2"
Weight: 282 lbs.
From: Toronto, Ontario, Canada
Finishing Move: Pumphandle Slam
Career Highlights: Hardcore Champion

BIOGRAPHY

It's hard to believe that Test is still a newcomer to the World Wrestling Federation. In the short time that Test has been with us, he's served as a prominent member of the Corporation and had the romance of the millennium with his almost-bride, Stephanie McMahon.

During the course of a few months, Test had to overcome more obstacles than one can imagine in his bid for Stephanie's love. Shane McMahon, the Mean Street Posse and the British Bulldog all stood in the young couple's way at one point during their courtship, but Test found a way to defeat them all. In doing so, the young Canadian impressed legions of Federation fans (especially the ladies) and officials as well.

Showing a tremendous amount of skill in the ring and natural talent as an entertainer outside of it, Test gave everyone associated with the W another reason to be excited about the future.

When Stephanie turned her back on him, it might have sent his world crashing down, but it certainly did not finish him off. The young Canadian with a tremendous amount of athletic ability and impressive physique has a very long future in the World Wrestling Federation!

ACTION	Moves	CONTROL
Facing the Opponent		
Irish Whip to Ropes		●
Falling Neckbreaker		↓+●
Side Buster		←+●
Stomach Crusher		↑+●
Suplex		→+●
Chop		✕
Big Boot		↓+✕
Toe Kick		←+✕
Clothesline		↑+✕
Austin Punches		→+✕
Facing the Groggy Opponent		
Falling Power Slam		↓+●
Falling Neckbreaker		←+●
Test Neck Breaker		↑+●
Small Package		→+●
Behind the Opponent		
Irish Whip to Ropes		●
Full Nelson Slam		↓+●
Pump Handle Slam		←+●
Sleeper Hold		↑+●
Pumphandle Drop		→+●
Opponent on Mat		
Upper Body		
Raise Opponent		●
Camel Clutch		↑+●
Mounted Punch		→+●
Mounted Punch		←+●
Angry Stomp		✕
Elbow Drop		↓+✕
Angry Stomp		←+✕
Elbow Drop		↑+✕
Angry Stomp		→+✕
Lower Body		
Raise Opponent		●
Leg Lock		↑+●
Kick to Leg		→+●
Boston Crab		←+●
Turnbuckle Moves		
Facing Opponent		
Irish Whip to Ropes		●
10 Punch		←+●/→+●
Mudhole Stomping		↓+●/↑+●
Behind Opponent		
Irish Whip to Ropes		●
Super Back Drop		←+●/→+●
Super Back Drop		↓+●/↑+●
Opponent Sitting in Lower Turnbuckle		
Raise Opponent		●
Foot Choke		←+●/→+●
Foot Choke		↓+●/↑+●
Power Clothesline		▲+✕
Turnbuckle Attacks		
Opponent Standing		
Double Axe Handle		✕
Flying Clothesline		←+✕/→+✕
Flying Clothesline		↓+✕/↑+✕
Opponent on Mat		
Test Diving Elbow		✕
Knee Drop		←+✕/→+✕
Knee Drop		↓+✕/↑+✕
Running Attacks		
Facing Opponent		
Neckbreaker		●
Neckbreaker Drop		←+●/→+●
Neckbreaker Drop		↓+●/↑+●
Power Clothesline		✕
Yakuza Kick		←+✕/→+✕
Yakuza Kick		↓+✕/↑+✕
Behind Opponent		
Bulldog		●
Bulldog		←+●/→+●
Bulldog		↓+●/↑+●
Running Counterattacks—Opponent Running		
Shoulder Back Toss		●
Powerslam		←+●/→+●
Powerslam		↓+●/↑+●

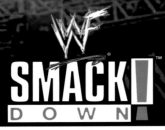

DID YOU KNOW?

Growing up, Test played hockey and went to school with NHL star Eric Lindro

Mudhole Stomp

↓+● / ↑+●

in front of a groggy oppo

Pumphandle Slam

←+●

from behind
an opponent

Full Nelson S

↓+●

behind an opponent

Diving Powerbomb

L1

TEST

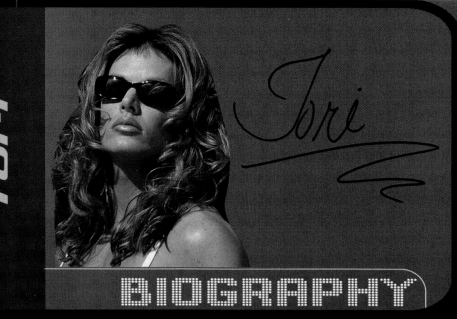

Tori

BIOGRAPHY

Enigmatic. Appealing. Mysterious. Powerful.

Sometimes looks can be very deceiving. Although Tori is one of the more tantalizing sights the World Wrestling Federation has to offer, you should never feel 100 percent secure in her presence.

Tori entered the WF as a result of her extreme admiration for one of its Superstars. Proving that she would do anything to earn attention from the object of her desire, Tori never tired of her efforts.

Later on down the road, Tori was locked in a number of legendary battles with Ivory over the World Wrestling Federation's Women's Championship. "Evening Gown" matches, Hardcore rules, whatever the stipulation, she was always up for the occasion.

Then came her interesting relationship with Kane.

Throughout all of her turns in the road, Tori has displayed one quality that has remained consistent—she is willing to do whatever it takes to achieve her goals. With her enticing physical appeal and the intelligence to match, Tori usually finds a way to get what she wants!

ACTION	Moves	CONTROL
Facing the Opponent		
Irish Whip to Ropes		●
Club to Neck		↓+●
Snapmare		←+●
Scoop Slam		↑+●
Snapmare		→+●
Middle Kick		×
Dropkick		↓+×
Slap		←+×
Double Axe Handle		↑+×
Back Elbow Smash		→+×
Facing the Groggy Opponent		
DDT		↓+●
Suplex		←+●
Small Package		↑+●
Suplex		→+●
Behind the Opponent		
Irish Whip to Ropes		●
Reverse Pin		↓+●
Turn to Face		←+●
Reverse Pin		↑+●
Turn to Face		→+●
Opponent on Mat		
Upper Body		
Raise Opponent		●
Sleeper Hold		↑+●
Knee Smash		→+●
Knee Smash		←+●
Angry Stomp		×
Angry Stomp		↓+×
Angry Stomp		←+×
Angry Stomp		↑+×
Angry Stomp		→+×
Lower Body		
Raise Opponent		●
Knee Stomp		↑+●
Leg Lock		→+●
Leg Lock		←+●
Turnbuckle Moves		
Facing Opponent		
Irish Whip to Ropes		●
Choke		←+●/→+●
Shoulder Thrusts		↓+●/↑+●
Behind Opponent		
Irish Whip to Ropes		●
School Boy		←+●/→+●
School Boy		↓+●/↑+●
Opponent Sitting in Lower Turnbuckle		
Raise Opponent		●
Choke		←+●/→+●
Choke		↓+●/↑+●
Shoulder Block		▲+×
Turnbuckle Attacks		
Opponent Standing		
Double Axe Handle		×
Missile Dropkick		←+×/→+×
Missile Dropkick		↓+×/↑+×
Opponent on Mat		
Elbow Drop		×
Knee Drop		←+×/→+×
Knee Drop		↓+×/↑+×
Running Attacks		
Facing Opponent		
Neckbreaker		●
Rolling Clutch Pin		←+●/→+●
Rolling Clutch Pin		↓+●/↑+●
Shoulder Block		×
Dropkick		←+×/→+×
Dropkick		↓+×/↑+×
Behind Opponent		
Bulldog		●
Bulldog		←+●/→+●
Bulldog		↓+●/↑+●
Running Counter Attacks—Opponent Running		
Monkey Toss		●
Shoulder Back Toss		←+●/→+●
Shoulder Back Toss		↓+●/↑+●

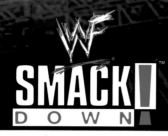
DID YOU KNOW?

Tori had only a handful of matches under her belt when WWF officials decided to give her a shot at the WWF Women's Championship—oh, did we forget to mention that it was at the biggest event of them all, WrestleMania® XV!

Snapmare
→+●

in front of opponent

Shoulder Back Toss
↓+●/←+●/→+●/↑+●

against a
running opponent

Missile Dropkick
↓+●/←+●/→+●/↑+●

diving from the turnbuckle

Tori Suplex
L1

Tori™

Triple H

Height: 6'4"
Weight: 246 lbs.
From: Greenwich, CT
Favorite Quote: "I am the Game!"
Finishing Move: Pedigree
Career Highlights: World Wrestling Federation Champion, Intercontinental Champion, European Champion, 1997 King of the Ring®

BIOGRAPHY

Perhaps when utilizing the Create a Superstar feature in W SmackDown!™, you should use Triple H as the mold. He embodies all that a World Wrestling Federation Superstar of this era should be.

He is in peak physical condition and dedicates himself to the gym so he remains that way. His technical ability is up there with the best of them, but if a match calls for him to brawl in the back with garbage cans and broomsticks—bring it on.

As far as his ability to entertain is concerned, one minute he'll have you rolling on the floor in a fit of hysteria because he just led an attack on a cross-town live event. The next minute you'll be throwing things at the television hoping that somehow, one of them will get through and hit him because he just got done insulting you before he screwed your favorite Superstar out of a win. He's intelligent, articulate, witty, and armed with an immeasurable amount of charisma.

And let's not forget the cool factor. With the rest of D-Generation X by his side, Triple H lives life in the World Wrestling Federation as a rock star who isn't going to let any set of rules run his game. Life on the edge is what it's all about for Triple H and his D-Generate pals.

Moves	
ACTION	**CONTROL**
Facing the Opponent	
Irish Whip to Ropes	●
Knee Smash	↓+●
Scoop Slam	←+●
Eye Rake	↑+●
Arm Wrench	→+●
Snap Jab	✕
Clothesline	↓+✕
Toe Kick	←+✕
Elbow Smash	↑+✕
Chop	→+✕
Facing the Groggy Opponent	
Rib Breaker	↓+●
Jumping Arm Breaker	←+●
Reverse Suplex	↑+●
Manhattan Drop	→+●
Behind the Opponent	
Irish Whip to Ropes	●
Diving Reverse DDT	↓+●
Back Drop	←+●
Dragon Sleeper	↑+●
Turn to Face	→+●
Opponent on Mat	
Upper Body	
Raise Opponent	●
Reverse Chin Lock	↑+●
Knee Smash	→+●
Mounted Punch	←+●
Angry Stomp	✕
Double Knee Drop	↓+✕
Angry Stomp	←+✕
Double Knee Drop	↑+✕
Angry Stomp	→+✕
Lower Body	
Raise Opponent	●
Figure 4 Leg Lock	↑+●
Kick to Leg	→+●
Knee Stomp	←+●
Turnbuckle Moves	
Facing Opponent	
Irish Whip to Ropes	●
Superplex	←+●/→+●
Shoulder Thrusts	↓+●/↑+●
Behind Opponent	
Irish Whip to Ropes	●
Super Back Drop	←+●/→+●
Super Back Drop	↓+●/↑+●
Opponent Sitting in Lower Turnbuckle	
Raise Opponent	●
Foot Choke	←+●/→+●
Foot Choke	↓+●/↑+●
Jumping Knee Attack	▲+✕
Turnbuckle Attacks	
Opponent Standing	
Double Axe Handle	✕
Flying Clothesline	←+✕/→+✕
Flying Clothesline	↓+✕/↑+✕
Opponent on Mat	
Knee Drop	✕
Knee Drop	←+✕/→+✕
Knee Drop	↓+✕/↑+✕
Running Attacks	
Facing Opponent	
Neckbreaker	●
Spear	←+●/→+●
Spear	↓+●/↑+●
Jumping Knee Attack	✕
Clothesline	←+✕/→+✕
Clothesline	↓+✕/↑+✕
Behind Opponent	
School Boy	●
School Boy	←+●/→+●
School Boy	↓+●/↑+●
Running Counterattacks—Opponent Running	
Monkey Toss	●
Shoulder Back Toss	←+●/→+●
Shoulder Back Toss	↓+●/↑+●

Double Knee Dr

↓+✕/↑+✕

with opponent on ma

Super Back Drop

↓+●/←+●/→+●/↑+●

from behind an opponent turnbuckle

Arm Wrenc

→+●

in front of opponen

Pedigree

L1

Undertaker

Moves		
ACTION		**CONTROL**
Facing the Opponent		
Irish Whip to Ropes		●
Shoulder Breaker		↓+●
DDT		←+●
Club to Neck		↑+●
Hard Scoop Slam		→+●
Throat Thrust		✕
Back Elbow Smash		↓+✕
Toe Kick		←+✕
Double Axe Handle		↑+✕
Austin Punches		→+✕
Facing the Groggy Opponent		
Jackknife Powerbomb		↓+●
DDT		←+●
Chokeslam		↑+●
Rib Breaker		→+●
Behind the Opponent		
Irish Whip to Ropes		●
Pumphandle Slam		↓+●
Diving Reverse DDT		←+●
Sleeper Hold		↑+●
Atomic Drop		→+●
Opponent on Mat		
Upper Body		
Raise Opponent		●
Mounted Punch		↑+●
Sleeper Hold		→+●
Darkness Choke		←+●
Angry Stomp		✕
Leg Drop		↓+✕
Knee Drop		←+✕
Elbow Drop		↑+✕
Knee Drop		→+✕
Lower Body		
Raise Opponent		●
Kick to Leg		↑+●
Knee Stomp		→+●
Knee Stomp		←+●
Turnbuckle Moves		
Facing Opponent		
Irish Whip to Ropes		●
Walk on the Rope		←+●/→+●
Choke		↓+●/↑+●
Behind Opponent		
Irish Whip to Ropes		●
Super Back Drop		←+●/→+●
Super Back Drop		↓+●/↑+●
Opponent Sitting in Lower Turnbuckle		
Raise Opponent		●
Choke		←+●/→+●
Choke		↓+●/↑+●
Flying Lariat		▲+✕
Turnbuckle Attacks		
Opponent Standing		
Double Axe Handle		✕
Flying Clothesline		←+✕/→+✕
Flying Clothesline		↓+✕/↑+✕
Opponent on Mat		
Knee Drop		✕
Knee Drop		←+✕/→+✕
Knee Drop		↓+✕/↑+✕
Running Attacks		
Facing Opponent		
Neckbreaker		●
Running DDT		←+●/→+●
Running DDT		↓+●/↑+●
Flying Lariat		✕
Diving Shoulder		←+✕/→+✕
Diving Shoulder		↓+✕/↑+✕
Behind Opponent		
Bulldog		●
Bulldog		←+●/→+●
Bulldog		↓+●/↑+●
Running Counterattacks—Opponent Running		
Monkey Toss		●
Shoulder Back Toss		←+●/→+●
Shoulder Back Toss		↓+●/↑+●

Height: 6'10"
Weight: 328 lbs.
From: Death Valley
Favorite Quote: "Rest in Peace!"
Finishing Move: Tombstone Piledriver
Career Highlights: World Wrestling
Federation Champion,
Tag Team Champion

BIOGRAPHY

What is it about the Undertaker that has kept him on top of the World Wrestling Federation for more than a decade? He's dark, mysterious, and evil, yet millions of fans around the world continue to be dedicated "creatures of the night" after all this time. In an age where everything seems to move at the speed of light. Not only has The Phenom remained, he's thrived throughout his illustrious career as a sports-entertainer.

From the early days of the urn and Paul Bearer to the more recent Corporate Ministry, the Undertaker has remained one of the most entertaining Superstars on the roster. With an entrance that few can rival, a commanding aura that surrounds his silence, and the maneuverability of a Superstar half his size, the Undertaker is the perfect mixture of entertainment and athleticism. Who could imagine a man taller than 6'10" walking on the top rope as if he were the highwire act in the traveling circus?

Let's not forget about power. Whether it's a "Tombstone Piledriver" or a hellacious choke slam, the Undertaker has more than one way to ensure that his opponent will "Rest in Peace!"

DID YOU KNOW?
The Undertaker was originally brought into the WF by Brother Love.

Darkness Choke
←+●

with opponent on mat

Pumphandle Slam
↓+●

behind the opponent

Walk on the Rope
←+●/→+●

opponent in turnbuckle

Tombstone Piledriver
[L1]

UNDERTAKER

Val Venis

Height: 6'4"
Weight: 245 lbs.
From: Las Vegas, NV
Favorite Quote: "Hello, Ladies!"
Finishing Move: Money Shot
Career Highlights: Intercontinental
Champion, European Champion

BIOGRAPHY

Anyone who owns a copy of WWF SmackDown!™ will have no problem keeping the game going all night long...but Val Venis doesn't have to plug anything in to keep his game of SmackDown! going all night long!

That is the essence of Val Venis. Armed with the virility of a mid-size army, the Big Valbowski is ready to take on all comers. If sexual conquests were a race, Val would be a marathon runner while the rest of the male species would be competing in the 40-yard dash.

Perhaps the most amazing thing about Val Venis though, is that he's always getting the best-looking ladies, despite the fact that he treats them like dirt! The Big Valbowski has never hidden his lack of respect toward the fairer sex, yet they can't seem to get enough of him. Val has had trysts with just about every hottie who has ever appeared in the World Wrestling Federation and, as if following a formula, he gets rid of them when he's had enough. And as soon as he unloads one, another is right around the corner!

Despite all of this extracurricular activity, Val Venis always has more than enough energy for the squared circle. A skilled athlete, Val also has the power and toughness to brawl it out with the best of them!

Moves	
ACTION	**CONTROL**
Facing the Opponent	
Irish Whip to Ropes	●
Arm Wrench	↓+●
DDT	←+●
Eye Rake	↑+●
Scissors Sweep	→+●
Chop	✕
Clothesline	↓+✕
Austin Punches	←+✕
Double Axe Handle	↑+✕
Elbow Smash	→+✕
Facing the Groggy Opponent	
Fisherman Suplex	↓+●
Double Arm Suplex	←+●
Stomach Crusher	↑+●
Spinebuster	→+●
Behind the Opponent	
Irish Whip to Ropes	●
Atomic Drop	↓+●
Russian Leg Sweep	←+●
Octopus Stretch	↑+●
German Suplex Pin	→+●
Opponent on Mat	
Upper Body	
Raise Opponent	●
Sleeper Hold	↑+●
Reverse Chin Lock	→+●
Mounted Punch	←+●
Angry Stomp	✕
Elbow Drop	↓+✕
Angry Stomp	←+✕
Elbow Drop	↑+✕
Angry Stomp	→+✕
Lower Body	
Raise Opponent	●
Kick to Groin	↑+●
Kick to Leg	→+●
Leg Lock	←+●
Turnbuckle Moves	
Facing Opponent	
Irish Whip to Ropes	●
Superplex	←+●/→+●
Mudhole Stomping	↓+●/↑+●
Behind Opponent	
Irish Whip to Ropes	●
Super Back Drop	←+●/→+●
Super Back Drop	↓+●/↑+●
Opponent Sitting in Lower Turnbuckle	
Raise Opponent	●
Foot Choke	←+●/→+●
Foot Choke	↓+●/↑+●
Back Elbow Attack	▲+✕
Turnbuckle Attacks	
Opponent Standing	
Double Axe Handle	✕
Double Axe Handle	←+✕/→+✕
Double Axe Handle	↓+✕/↑+✕
Opponent on Mat	
Elbow Drop	✕
Knee Drop	←+✕/→+✕
Knee Drop	↓+✕/↑+✕
Running Attacks	
Facing Opponent	
Neckbreaker Drop	●
Neckbreaker	←+●/→+●
Neckbreaker	↓+●/↑+●
Back Elbow Attack	✕
Shoulder Block	←+✕/→+✕
Shoulder Block	↓+✕/↑+✕
Behind Opponent	
School Boy	●
School Boy	←+●/→+●
School Boy	↓+●/↑+●
Running Counterattacks—Opponent Running	
Monkey Toss	●
Pulling Walk Slam	←+●/→+●
Pulling Walk Slam	↓+●/↑+●

DID YOU KNOW?

Of all Val Venis' loves, his love for politics may be the strongest.

Scissors Sweep

→ + ●

in front of opponent

German Suplex Pin

→ + ●

in front of opponent

Neckbreaker Drop

●

running at an opponent

The Money Shot

L1

your opponent must be on the mat
from turnbuckle

VALVENIS

HEELLOOOO, LADIEEESSS!

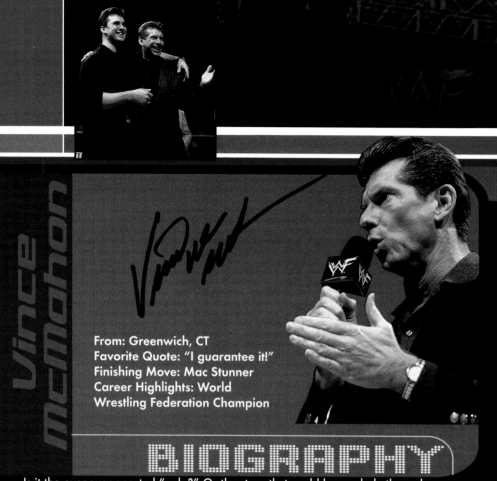

Vince McMahon

From: Greenwich, CT
Favorite Quote: "I guarantee it!"
Finishing Move: Mac Stunner
Career Highlights: World
Wrestling Federation Champion

BIOGRAPHY

Is it the over-exaggerated "gulp?" Or the stare that could burn a hole through the ozone layer? Perhaps it's the way his voice gets all scratchy when he screams, "You sonuvabitch!" Odds are it's a combination off all three, along with all of his other unique traits and abilities, that has earned Vince McMahon a permanent spot in the emotional vault of millions of fans around the world. Love him or hate him, with arrogance, perseverance and great facial expressions, the distinguished owner of the World Wrestling Federation has become a central figure on WF television.

But don't let his dapper exterior or mental acumen trick you into thinking Mr. McMahon is a pushover in the ring. Armed with an unbelievable desire to destroy his opponents—in the business world and between the ropes—Mr. McMahon has been involved in some of the most intense contests Federation fans have ever witnessed. Unfortunately for the owner, he's usually on the receiving end of much of this intensity!

Look over Mr. McMahon's competitive resume and you'll see a *Royal Rumble*® victory, a fall from the top of a steel cage, a win (along with Shane) over Stone Cold Steve Austin in a handicap ladder match, and an unforgettable war with Triple H. Every time Mr. McMahon steps in the ring you can be certain that he'll give his all to ensure that you're entertained.

The only question that remains is, where has Mr. McMahon kicked more butt...in the office or in the ring?!

ACTION	Moves	CONTROL
Facing the Opponent		
Irish Whip to Ropes		●
Eye Rake		↓+●
Club to Neck		←+●
Eye Rake		↑+●
Arm Wrench		→+●
Austin Punches		✕
Double Axe Handle		↓+✕
Chop		←+✕
Double Axe Handle		↑+✕
Toe Kick		→+✕
Facing the Groggy Opponent		
Piledriver		↓+●
Club to Neck		←+●
Side Buster		↑+●
Arm Wrench		→+●
Behind the Opponent		
Irish Whip to Ropes		●
Turn Facing Front		↓+●
Turn Facing Front		←+●
Turn Facing Front		↑+●
Turn Facing Front		→+●
Opponent on Mat		
Upper Body		
Raise Opponent		●
Sleeper Hold		↑+●
Knee Smash		→+●
Knee Smash		←+●
Angry Stomp		✕
Angry Stomp		↓+✕
Angry Stomp		←+✕
Angry Stomp		↑+✕
Angry Stomp		→+✕
Lower Body		
Raise Opponent		●
Knee Stomp		↑+●
Kick to Leg		→+●
Leg Lock		←+●
Turnbuckle Moves		
Facing Opponent		
Irish Whip to Ropes		●
Shoulder Thrusts		←+●/→+●
Mudhole Stomping		↓+●/↑+●
Behind Opponent		
Irish Whip to Ropes		●
Super Back Drop		←+●/→+●
Super Back Drop		↓+●/↑+●
Opponent Sitting in Lower Turnbuckle		
Raise Opponent		●
Choke		←+●/→+●
Choke		↓+●/↑+●
Shoulder Block		▲+✕
Turnbuckle Attacks		
Opponent Standing		
Double Axe Handle		✕
Double Axe Handle		←+✕/→+✕
Double Axe Handle		↓+✕/↑+✕
Opponent on Mat		
Knee Drop		✕
Elbow Drop		←+✕/→+✕
Elbow Drop		↓+✕/↑+✕
Running Attacks		
Facing Opponent		
Neckbreaker		●
Neckbreaker		←+●/→+●
Neckbreaker		↓+●/↑+●
Shoulder Block		✕
Shoulder Block		←+✕/→+✕
Shoulder Block		↓+✕/↑+✕
Behind Opponent		
Bulldog		●
Bulldog		←+●/→+●
Bulldog		↓+●/↑+●
Running Counterattacks—Opponent Running		
Monkey Toss		●
Shoulder Back Toss		←+●/→+●
Shoulder Back Toss		↓+●/↑+●

DID YOU KNOW?

In the little free time that he has, Vince likes to ride his motorcycle through the beautiful Connecticut countryside.

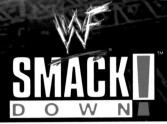

Sleeper Hol

↑+●

opponent on the ground

Arm Wrench

→+●

in front of opponent

Leg Lock

←+●

with opponent on ma

Stunner

L1

Vince McMahon™

X-Pac

Height: 6'
Weight: 212 lbs.
From: Minneapolis, MN
Favorite Quote: "Your ass is grass, and I'm gonna smoke it!"
Finishing Move: X-Factor
Career Highlights: European Champion, Tag Team Champion

BIOGRAPHY

Sometimes, timing is everything.

Just as Triple H decided he needed to recreate D-Generation X, X-Pac was able to return to the World Wrestling Federation. Not only did this give X-Pac the opportunity to work with one of his closest friends, but it also put him in the perfect situation. X-Pac personified all that DX stood for.

Packed with an enormous amount of energy, the Minnesota native is always moving in hyper-speed. Because he's never one to listen to authority, you know X-Pac is ready to stir the pot the second his music hits. With an entrance comparable to that of a rock star, X-Pac jumps around the ring and screams his head off while pyro explodes behind him.

Although not one of the biggest Superstars to ever grace the squared circle, X-Pac refuses to back down from any challenges. In fact, if there is one criticism about X-Pac, it's that his heart is too big. Choosing not to acknowledge his size disadvantage in many matches, X-Pac proves the age-old saying, "It's not the size of the dog in the fight, but the size of the fight in the dog."

ACTION	Moves	CONTROL
Facing the Opponent		
Irish Whip to Ropes		●
Headlock and Punch		↓+●
Snapmare		←+●
Eye Rake		↑+●
DDT		→+●
Middle Kick		✕
Spinning to Face X-Pac		↓+✕
Snap Jab		←+✕
Spinning Wheel Kick		↑+✕
Spinning Kick		→+✕
Facing the Groggy Opponent		
Piledriver		↓+●
Spinning Back Drop		←+●
Hurracanrana		↑+●
Fisherman Suplex		→+●
Behind the Opponent		
Irish Whip to Ropes		●
Reverse Pin		↓+●
Back Drop		←+●
School Boy		↑+●
Turn to Face		→+●
Opponent on Mat		
Upper Body		
Raise Opponent		●
Knee Smash		↑+●
Sleeper Hold		→+●
Mounted Punch		←+●
Angry Stomp		✕
Angry Stomp		↓+✕
Leg Drop		←+✕
Angry Stomp		↑+✕
Leg Drop		→+✕
Lower Body		
Raise Opponent		●
Kick to Leg		↑+●
Kick to Groin		→+●
Knee Stomp		←+●
Turnbuckle Moves		
Facing Opponent		
Irish Whip to Ropes		●
10 Punch		←+●/→+●
Mudhole Stomping		↓+●/↑+●
Behind Opponent		
Irish Whip to Ropes		●
Super Back Drop		←+●/→+●
Super Back Drop		↓+●/↑+●
Opponent Sitting in Lower Turnbuckle		
Raise Opponent		●
Foot Choke		←+●/→+●
Foot Choke		↓+●/↑+●
Bronco Buster		▲+✕
Turnbuckle Attacks		
Opponent Standing		
Double Axe Handle		✕
Spinning Wheel Kick		←+✕/→+✕
Spinning Wheel Kick		↓+✕/↑+✕
Opponent on Mat		
Knee Drop		✕
Knee Drop		←+✕/→+✕
Knee Drop		↓+✕/↑+✕
Running Attacks		
Facing Opponent		
Neckbreaker		●
Neckbreaker		←+●/→+●
Neckbreaker		↓+●/↑+●
Flying Lariat		✕
Bronco Buster		←+✕/→+✕
Bronco Buster		↓+✕/↑+✕
Behind Opponent		
School Boy		●
School Boy		←+●/→+●
School Boy		↓+●/↑+●
Running Counterattacks—Opponent Running		
Monkey Toss		●
Pulling Walk Slam		←+●/→+●
Pulling Walk Slam		↓+●/↑+●

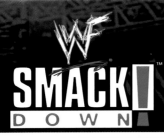

DID YOU KNOW?

During his first stretch with the WWF, X-Pac (then the Kid) pulled one of the biggest upsets in World Wrestling Federation history by defeating Scott Hall—after which he became known as the 1-2-3 Kid (for registering the three-count on his nemesis).

Spinning to Face X-Pac

↓+X

in front of an opponent

DDT

→+●

in front of opponent

Spinning Wheel Kick

↓+X/←+X/→+X/↑+X

from the turnbuckle

X-Factor

L1

X-PAC

"The most electrifying wrestling game the world has ever seen!" —GameFan

Thousands of signature moves, taunts and mannerisms

Complete Create-A-Wrestler Mode—assign individual moves, costumes and fighting styles

Tons of game modes, including Cage Match, Road to WrestleMania, Create-A-PPV.

"The biggest, baddest, meanest, fattest, coolest, raddest wrestling game in the known universe." —Nintendo Power

WrestleMania XIV
In an epic contest, Stone Cold Steve Austin becomes World Champion with a w... over Shawn Michael...

WrestleMania XII
Heartbreak Kid Shawn Michaels wins a 60 minute Iron Man match for the title

WrestleMania X
Shawn Michaels and Razor Ramon wrestle for the IC Strap in an original hardcore classic

WrestleMania VIII
Shawn Michaels and the Undertaker continue their rise to the top with wins

WrestleMania VI
The tide turns as both Mega Powers lose in the same night

WrestleMania IV
Plays host to the first WrestleMania Heavy weight title tournament

WrestleMania 2
The first WrestleMania battle royal

85 86 87 88 89 90 91 92 93 94 95 96 97

WrestleMania I
World Wrestling Federation® ushers in a new age of wrestling popularity

WrestleMania III
Breaks live attendance records with a capacity crowd

WrestleMania V
Shawn Michaels' WrestleMania debut as a member of The Rockers™

WrestleMania VII
The Undertaker scores a decisive victory in his WrestleMania debut

WrestleMania IX
Federation Championship changes hands twice in one night

WrestleMania XI
X-Pac™ and Road Dogg™ make their WrestleMania debuts as ringside support for Jeff Jarrett™ and Razor Ramon™

WrestleMania 13
The Undertaker begins his second Federation Championship reign with a main event victory

STEVE AUSTIN

entrances complete with Titantron™ and theme mus...

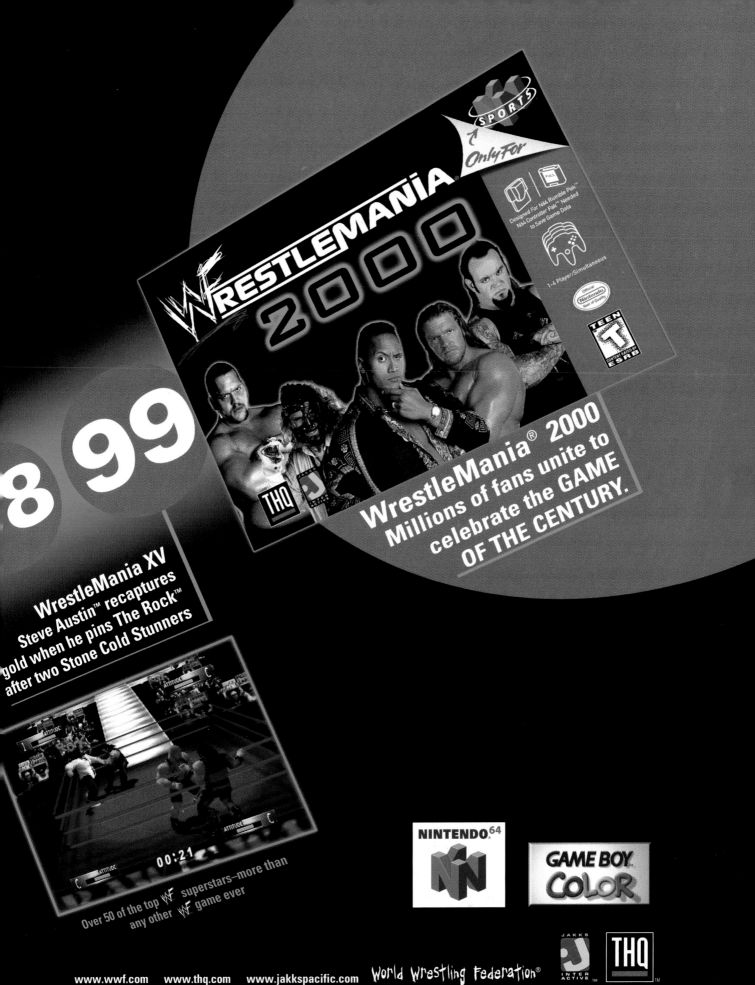

THE PERFECT RECIPE FOR MILLENNIUM MADNESS.
WRESTLEMANIA® 2000

TITANTRON LIVE SERIES 3

ATTITUDE RING™

TITANTRON LIVE

1 2 PIECE™

PUT IT IN THE MIX

MIX IN EQUAL PARTS of RAGE AND CARNAGE. BLEND WITH A HEAPING DOSE of REVENGE. ADD A DASH of TRASH TALKIN'. THEN SERVE.

WRESTLEMANIA   JAKKS Pacific inc.

World Wrestling Federation®

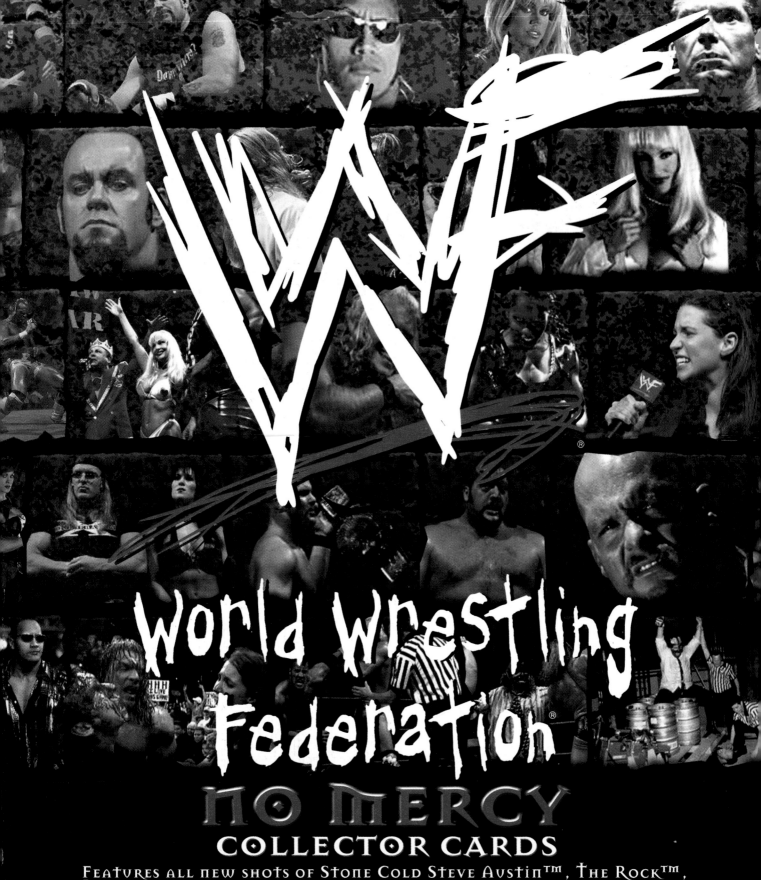

World Wrestling Federation®

no mercy

COLLECTOR CARDS

FEATURES ALL NEW SHOTS OF STONE COLD STEVE AUSTIN™, THE ROCK™, TRIPLE H™, MANKIND™ AND ALL THE WORLD WRESTLING FEDERATION® SUPERSTARS, IN THEIR MOST OUTRAGEOUS HARDCORE MATCHES.

- 81-CARD FOIL STAMPED SERIES ON SILVERCOAT STOCK
- 6 RANDOMLY INSERTED PIECE OF THE RING MEMORABILIA CHASE CARDS
- 7 HOLOGRAPHIC HARDCORE CHAMPION CHASE CARDS